Thanks

We wish to thank TTI Performance Systems, Ltd. TTI's assessment tools form the basis for the content of this book. In particular, we thank Anne Klink for her comments and assistance.

We also wish to thank our peers, clients and friends who gave the time to read and critique our proof copies and provide feedback.

Special Thanks for the Inspiration:

Before his sudden passing, John inspired and assisted us with this project, and we miss him. Thanks for leaving us these kind words.

> *"I have read every word, every line, every page of your book draft and would like to congratulate you on a fine piece of work. The story kept me engaged throughout with a nice piece of intrigue with an 'Ah ha' moment at the end that made me think, 'Good on ya!'"*

John Butler, 1955 – 2010 - Century Management, Dublin, Ireland

John was a world leader in business consulting. He and his wife, Imelda, developed many personal development programs that are still being used the world over. Everyone who knew him sadly misses him. He was a great inspiration in the development of this book.

MARK
Great To Get Togothu

[signature]

Layton and Myrna, I consider us great friends. Here is my endorsement for you. Serve greatly with love all who listen and chose to apply the principles.
—Mark Victor Hansen, Newport Beach, CA
Author of *Chicken Soup for the Soul*

MYRNA PARK, MARK VICTOR HANSEN, AND LAYTON PARK

I have done business with Layton and Myrna for thirty years and use their services often. I really appreciate their commonsense approach to business. The tools they talk about in the story are really amazing.
—Dennis Dale, Owner
Wayne Manufacturing
and Trend Home Improvement

The first time I read this story I thought, How do you know so much about my life? *As the owner of a mechanical company it surprised me that an author would understand so many of the problems in our industry. I am looking forward to the next book in the series.*

—Blair Husak, Owner
Mechanical Service Company, Kelowna, BC

I refer to Layton as "The Business Builder," because I think he uses the planning skills he learned when he studied architecture.

—Morley Muldoon
Morley Muldoon Transport Ltd., Wainwright, AB

What a great book! Valuable insights and practical information that every manager and business owner should have—all packaged in an interesting, engaging, easy-to-read story. You have a wonderful style and do a great job with the storytelling and the dialogue. I also really enjoyed the little twist at the end.
Great work.

—Jacquelyn Freedman
TimeWorks Consulting LLC, Milford, NJ

I bought your book Get Out of Your Way *about two years ago when I was residing and working in Ankara at Estonian Embassy.*
Your book gave me so much encouragement, and I wish to thank you for that!
Since my first encounter with your book, I have been through dramatic changes—I divorced my wife, resigned as a diplomat from the Estonian Foreign Ministry, became an entrepreneur, and moved from Ankara to Istanbul rather than going back to my home country immediately.
I explained to you what I did this year to show you that my confidence in dealing with myself, people, and projects has grown significantly and I am on a path of steady growth. I am happier than ever because of those changes in my mentality. I would say your book unleashed the real me inside.
I remain thankful to you what for what you taught me!

—Vahur Luhtsalu
Estonian diplomat
Istanbul, Turkey

See more personal references and endorsements at the end of the book.

A SIMPLE BLUEPRINT FOR GETTING ALONG AT WORK

COMMUNICATION TOOLS FOR ANY TRADE

LAYTON PARK and MYRNA PARK

iUniverse, Inc.
Bloomington

COMMUNICATION TOOLS FOR ANY TRADE

A Simple Blueprint For Getting Along At Work

iUniverse books may be ordered through booksellers or by contacting:

iUniverse
1663 Liberty Drive
Bloomington, IN 47403
www.iuniverse.com
1-800-Authors (1-800-288-4677)

ISBN: 978-1-4759-6734-0 (sc)
ISBN: 978-1-4759-6733-3 (hc)
ISBN: 978-1-4759-6732-6 (e)

Library of Congress Control Number: 2013900789

Printed in the United States of America

iUniverse rev. date: 2/20/2013

ALSO BY LAYTON PARK ||||||||||||||||||||||||||||||||||||||||||||||||||||||||

Get Out of Your Way	Llewellyn Worldwide Ltd
Chicken Coop for a Rubber Sole	iUniverse, Inc.
Spirit Doctor	iUniverse, Inc.
If You Are Going to Lead … Don't Spit!	iUniverse, Inc.

Contents

INTRODUCTION

The entrepreneur is a risk taker who blazes new trails in business. However, there is a lot to be said for recognizing the paths of other trailblazers and incorporating myriad experiences into a dynamic business model.

With the combination of education and experience, an enthusiastic ingénue can transform the face of business while still relying on traditionally effective models.

This book will examine the styles of various leaders, how they communicate, and how to communicate more effectively with them.

Layton Park entered into business in 1975 with a design-build company, which quickly expanded to include over eighty direct employees and several subcontractors.

Myrna Park started a real estate company in 1985 that also quickly grew to become one of the leading companies in the area, employing over 25 percent of the real estate agents in her market.

In 1996 they sold both companies and began a company, Max-U.com Inc., and worked in association with Brian Tracy offering courses in personal development, sales, and leadership.

In 2000 they became certified with TTI of Scottsdale, Arizona, using their tools for assessing behavioural and motivational psychology.

Today Max-U.com Inc. works with organizations around North America, both small entrepreneurs and multinationals, as business analysts in the areas of strategic planning, communication, leadership, and succession planning.

Layton is a member of IIBA˚ and has the designation of Certified Business Analysis Professional™*.

Myrna and Layton are certified with TTI as Certified Professional Behaviour Analysts (CPBA) and Certified Professional Values Analysts (CPVA).

Myrna is also a Certified Professional TTI TriMetrix Analyst and a Certified Professional TTI DNA Analyst.

Today's entrepreneurs face stiff local competition, higher operating costs, more government regulations, big box stores, and offshore and online competitors, all a part of the new economy. Despite this competition, entrepreneurs are starting new businesses and succeeding.

Successful small business owners recognize the weaknesses of large companies and become more efficient in those areas. Nowhere is that more evident than in the trades. This story is about one such tradesman and his wife who started a small plumbing business out of necessity and succeeded only to find and conquer new challenges.

Large corporations are challenged to offer the personal service of smaller companies. They often cannot have the same person working with a customer from one contact to another, and the real decision maker is often not available to discuss any concerns with the clients. To overcome this disadvantage, larger companies have to ramp up their customer service levels and train service staff to engage with the customers, creating a sense of ownership and caring.

This was recently brought home to me when my air-conditioning quit working and the house became a boiler. I talked to the owner of a large local mechanical firm on Wednesday who said he could get someone to fix it right away. Friday I was told that they were backed up and it would have to be Monday. Early Monday morning a fellow showed up who said he had just completed his first-year apprenticeship and appeared somewhat unsure of himself. After two hours of talking on the phone to the service manager several times and testing everything, I was told that the compressors were burned out but should be covered by warranty. If so, the bill for the labour would only be $1,150.

The confidence of the fellow made me feel uneasy, so I called a referral for a one-man operator, who came over immediately to look at it and had it fixed within the hour for $110.

I know the owner of the first company is an honest, hard-working businessman who wants to offer great service, but in this case my referrals will go to the second company because the one-man operator doesn't have the people problems the bigger company does. This advantage, however, is also his disadvantage when it comes to bigger work or expanding his business.

Once we understand that both big and small business have advantages and disadvantages, we can identify our strengths and weaknesses and formulate a plan to capitalize on both.

Big-box stores have had a huge impact on business over the past few years, so smaller businesses have had to adapt in order to remain profitable.

Despite the doom and gloom presented daily in the media, there has never been a better time to be in business.

This book is how one man, Joe, faced the challenge of losing his job and turned it into an opportunity to create a successful new plumbing business. His small company grew quickly, expanding into similar products and services, such as heating, air conditioning, retail sales of plumbing and heating fixtures, and a separate service department, without the support of a franchise or a proven system to follow. Now Joe faces his biggest challenge.

This story has been drawn from our own experiences in starting and running businesses, from examples encountered in consulting with our clients, and from many of the programs developed to face such issues.

Using this wealth of resources as a foundation, Joe is able to overcome his problem. We trust this story will give you insight into how to creatively overcome the challenges in your own business, no matter what size or in what industry.

This book began as a serialized column created for a business magazine. The story was written to demonstrate some of the business and interpersonal skills and techniques Max-U has been using with clients across North America. We trust that using a story format will make the information more entertaining and memorable.

This particular book is about the plumbing and heating business, but the principles apply to all businesses. We want to thank many of our larger customers for helping launch this book by buying it in bulk to give as a gift to employees, suppliers, and associated businesses.

This story about Joe was in our public columns five years before the 2008 US presidential election made another "Joe the Plumber" famous; however, we decided that our Joe was too old to go through a name change.

We trust that you will find the information useful in further developing your business regardless of its size or its purpose.

Layton and Myrna
* IIBA˚, the IIBA˚ logo, BABOK˚ and Business Analysis Body of Knowledge˚ are registered trademarks owned by International Institute of Business Analysis.

These trademarks are used with permission of International Institute of Business Analysis.

TTI, Certified Professional Behaviour Analysts (CPBA), Certified Professional Values Analysts (CPVA), Certified Professional TTI TriMetrix* Analyst, and Certified Professional TTI DNA Analyst are all certifications granted by TTI Performance Systems, Ltd.

FIRE THE WIFE? ||||||||||||

"Fire Betty?" Joe muttered to himself. "I can't fire my own wife." Joe ran his fingers through his slightly greying thick hair. Although the dark black hair had seemed to fade a bit and the firm muscles he once had were now getting a little soft, he was still a good-looking man. It had been eighteen years since he started his plumbing business and eight since he last worked in the field himself. Despite his success, this was one of those times when he wished he were still on the tools working by himself, not having to deal with employees.

"How can I keep my employees from leaving?" The thought kept running through his mind. He not only needed the four managers who had given him this ultimatum, but he liked them and even understood their frustration. But asking him to choose between them and Betty was unbelievable.

"I thought I had faced just about every problem a businessman can face," he thought as he closed his eyes and leaned back into the comfortable reed chair. Joe was so wrapped up in thought that he didn't notice the white stucco wall behind him reflecting the warmth of the early spring sun. Nor had he seen the full palette of vibrant flowers surrounding the attractive deck at the Lakeview Resort. They sweetened the transition from the man-made structure to the soft and natural beauty of the surrounding grounds, lit by sunlight filtering down through the tall pines.

The magnificent jewel-like lake carved out of the rugged British Columbia landscape reflected the high hills and mountains, providing a surreal backdrop.

The sunshine warming the deck had long since melted the ice in Joe's tea. Still oblivious to the magnificence of the world around him, Joe continued to mull over this latest business challenge.

Joe had never planned to own his own business, but when the pulp mill closed and he couldn't find another job in town, he was faced with three options: find a different career, move to a job in another community, or start his own shop.

Joe had ruled out changing careers—he couldn't think of anything he would rather do. He was a journeyman plumber by trade and enjoyed the work.

Betty and he felt that they had invested years building a meaningful life with good friends and family here, so they were reluctant to move away. Nor could they agree on a place where they would prefer to live. Joe liked the small town and the closeness to the wilderness. He could be out hunting or fishing in just a few minutes. The winter offered excellent trails for riding his snow machine or cross-country skiing. He loved being able to walk down Main Street and talk to more than half the people he met or walk into the coffee shop and sit at a table full of other locals who always welcomed him.

Betty also had many good friends and now that they had been married for two years was beginning to think that this would be a great place to raise children.

There was no plumbing shop in town, and the community had come to depend on Joe to moonlight in the evenings and on weekends while working at the mill. The extra money had come in handy to pay down their mortgage and for the few toys a guy needed to enjoy the great outdoors. Joe had been so busy that he'd had to refer work to his coworkers, so he felt that the transition into his own plumbing business would be easy. Still, his thought was, he was a plumber, not a businessman, so he was reluctant to go out on his own.

Joe and Betty talked over the pros and cons and mostly the risks for several weeks before they finally decided that the right answer was to start their own business.

Joe spent the next several days trying to think up a unique and catchy name, but in the end he registered "Joe's Plumbing and Heating." He painted "A flush always beats a full house" on the side of his old van, along with his name and phone number, and he was in business.

Joe put in long hard days for the first three years, building the business and doing all the fieldwork. Betty kept her job as a bookkeeper for the tire store and then spent the evenings doing the books and paying the bills for the new business. At times it seemed as though they had given up all free time and were now slaves to the business. They loved the challenge and apparent independence of being their own boss.

The first few years presented more than their share of struggles with customers who took their time paying, suppliers who did not deliver when promised, and slow times when it seemed like no one needed their service. Joe was sure the bumps in the road would smooth out and it would soon be clear sailing all the way to the bank.

By the fourth year the business had grown to three employees and was beginning to provide a good living, so Betty gave up her day job. As the business only required her part-time, they felt it would be a good time to start a family.

The first daughter, Tracy, was followed a short year later by Janine. Betty enjoyed the freedom to spend a lot of time with the girls yet still be able to work three part days a week. Once the girls began school, the business had grown to six employees and Betty began spending more time in the business.

Suddenly it was eighteen years later, the girls were in their teens, and the business now had four strong departments. The first bumps and challenges had long since been smoothed out, and Betty now was the full-time office manager.

Over the years, as each challenge was overcome, it always seemed to be replaced with a new larger one. Although Joe and Betty were becoming richer on paper, rising inventory, the need for a physical location, more trucks, tools, new employees, and equipment, and the ever-increasing receivables offered new challenges that seemed to keep cash at bay.

Occasionally, Joe thought he would prefer to have his old job back at the mill with its regular hours, weekends off, paid holidays, routine work, steady paycheques, and no worries about cash flow, customers, employees, or suppliers.

Joe knew that his plumbing and heating business was providing him with a good life. The business had grown into a successful venture, thanks in large part to Betty's management and the life breathed into the town by a resort, convention centre, and a golf course, which had opened on the outskirts of the city ten years ago. The resort opened with a hundred rooms on the lake and began promoting abroad. It had been an immediate success, employing dozens of direct employees with numerous spin-off jobs. After only three years, they had added a number of cottages, creating more construction and resort positions.

Joe's Plumbing and Heating won a number of the resort's ongoing maintenance contracts. Joe's pricing was competitive due to the lower overhead of being local. Betty had a keen eye for controlling costs to ensure that the bottom line was always black.

They had kept the resort business all these years because of Joe's personal service and the relationships he always developed with his clients.

When the resort began building the cottages, it created a need for a small heating and air-conditioning contractor, and the growing population expanded the need for those services in town as well.

Joe hired Bob, an old buddy with the necessary trade tickets, to start the heating and air-conditioning division of the business.

The local economy continued to expand as other tourist services, such as houseboat rentals, evening lake cruises, waterskiing school, and local sightseeing flights, sprang up to service the resort's clients. A few years later a ski hill was built in the mountains just a few miles away, and the town continued to grow. As the demand for the plumbing and heating services grew, Joe bought the abandoned tire store at the end of Main Street. As the girls were now both in school, Betty began to work full-time.

Using the back of the building as a shop, Joe and Betty began filling the front with related retail products such as fireplaces, barbeques, and specialty kitchen and bath fixtures, finally expanding into a line of spas and pools as well. The business continued to be profitable for the next few years, but the need for more inventory taxed their cash flow. It seemed that the more successful they were, the more they had to borrow from the local bank.

With almost two dozen trades people employed, Joe promoted Frank, one of his plumbers, to manage the plumbing side, with Bob managing the heating and air-conditioning side of the business. Joe seemed to spend most his time sorting out problems, negotiating contracts, schmoozing customers, buying trucks and equipment, or going over financials with Betty and meeting with the company banker, accountant, and lawyer. He had struggled with the idea of giving up the tools and becoming a businessman as he still thought of himself as a plumber first, but all the other business demands seemed to take up most his time.

The business continued to grow, and the two department managers convinced Joe to hire Leigh as their first full-time salesperson so the business could promote more direct sales. The thought was that if they were going to install the fixtures anyway, why not have the customers buy them from them rather than bring them some third-party fixtures, many of which were cheap and created additional problems. They believed that it would not only make the company more profitable but would keep the customers happier as well. Joe finally agreed, and the decision turned out to be a good one.

Leigh became the front man for Joe's business, as he was present at every community event, especially anything to do with art or music. A good-looking and friendly person, Leigh was well-liked in the community and always well-dressed; he looked like a businessman.

Leigh immediately began making changes in the front office, building new displays that showcased the products and decorating the showroom to look more professional. Leigh modified his small drab office into a pleasant place to meet clients, with some colourful paintings of the area by local artists. Leigh seemed to have a steady stream of people coming in to visit him, and soon sales were rolling in faster than Joe had imagined.

As both retail sales and service increased, Joe promoted Leigh to the position of sales manager and put him in charge of finding new products as well as hiring and managing a new salesperson. As the business continued to grow, a second salesperson was added under Leigh to take on additional speciality products. Now the challenge was to keep all these people focused on the growing business and working together as a team.

That was when things started to come to a head. Joe became frustrated because a number of clients had expressed dissatisfaction with the company's service. With the building boom going on, new construction was keeping both the plumbing and heating divisions extremely busy. They hired a number of new young tradesmen, and their experienced people were promoted to keep the larger projects running smoothly. As a result, the smaller service and installation jobs began to take a backseat.

Joe tried to make the division managers see the importance of keeping all the customers happy, but they argued that they were busy ensuring that the bigger contracts ran smoothly and could not afford to take men away to deal with small warranty or repair issues. They were doing their best to balance all the jobs, and Joe understood the importance they gave the big jobs, as they were the main income for the company.

Sometimes Joe would leave the office to do an install or service job himself, but Betty would point out that this was not the best use of his time as he was more valuable securing more contracts and overseeing the general company operations.

The team continued to juggle schedules and try to fit in the smaller jobs, but this would upset some of the retail customers. Leigh began to complain at managers' meetings that his salespeople were losing sales because of a problem committing to a firm install date. Still they struggled on, continuing to grow despite the problems, until one Monday afternoon when Betty returned from the bank and called everyone to her office.

"Will this take long? I promised a contractor I'd have a price for him this afternoon," Frank said. He combed his hand through his graying blond hair from habit, and his mind seemed to be back in his office thinking about the work this meeting had taken him away from.

Both Leigh and Bob seemed to nod unconsciously in agreement as they sat down, as they too had several tasks waiting for completion.

Joe walked in last and looked around and then spoke to Betty as he closed the door. "What is going on?"

"I was totally embarrassed today, and I don't like it." Betty's voice was sharp as she sat up straight and looked around the room at the four men.

"I attended a chamber lunch today, and while we were networking before the lunch, Mrs. Schultz told me rather loudly that she was not happy with our service. Apparently, she was told that we would install her hot tub over two weeks ago, and she has not heard from us as to what is happening or why we have not shown up!" Betty looked first at Leigh and then at Frank.

"The real embarrassing part was that Mr. Howe was there and said he had the same problem a couple of months ago with the new air conditioner he had bought for his house. Said the hot days were almost done before it was in and working." This time her sharp eyes turned toward Bob, and he squirmed in his seat.

"I attend chamber meetings partly as a volunteer for the community and partly to network with other businesspeople and potential clients. If our reputation is that we offer this type of service, it is probably costing us business. We've always been proud of our service, and I don't like getting that kind of feedback. What are we going to do about it?"

The four men looked everywhere but directly at Betty, and it was Joe who spoke first.

"It's my fault." Joe shifted his weight from one leg to another like a schoolboy caught in a lie. He loved Betty dearly and he was the boss, but still, after all these years, when she became direct he felt uncomfortable, and it showed.

"I told Leigh that I thought we could fit that hot tub hook-up into the schedule, and we want to keep the Schultzes happy. Most of our men are tied up on the new strip mall project that Tom Schultz is project-managing for the owner. He does not want Frank to take anyone off his job as it is behind schedule." Joe was choosing his words carefully as he did not want this to sound like an excuse, yet it was the reason the job kept getting postponed.

"I told Tom that our other crews were equally backlogged. He said to put off the job at his home for a while and he would let his wife know. Maybe he thought it was easier to let her be angry with us than him." Joe flashed a weak smile.

It was Bob's turn to take the hot seat. "I had a similar problem on Howe's air conditioner. I couldn't shut down a big job for a day to send someone over to his home for the installation. This is becoming a problem. I try to fill in on the small jobs where I can, but you know that there is just not enough time in a week."

"Everyone in business has challenges." Betty's tone was lower and slower now as she surveyed all four men. "When it is busy like it is now, all businesses have these problems; when it is slow, everyone has different problems. When it rains, it rains on everyone's job. We are not unique. What sets apart the leading companies from the rest is not that they don't have problems, but they have a way to deal with the problems and minimize the effect." She paused and looked around, but no one spoke, so she continued.

"It seems to me that we are using avoidance techniques to deal with our problems, and I am not happy!" She let her voice rise a little at the end to emphasize her point. "So, gentlemen, what are we going to do?"

"I will try to get someone out to the Schultzes' tomorrow," Frank said.

"I have meetings in the afternoon, but if you give me someone in the morning, I can get them going," Joe said, looking at Frank.

Everyone but Betty seemed to shuffle in their chairs, feeling that the tension had been broken and they could soon get back to what they had been doing before the meeting.

"Not good enough!" Betty stated bluntly in the strong voice she reserved for when she meant business.

"First, let's review the word 'try.'" She paused again before continuing, "'Try' is asking for forgiveness before failure." She looked around the room again to ensure that she had everyone's attention. She then went on to explain.

"If I say I will 'try' to meet you for lunch tomorrow, and then I don't show up, you can't be angry with me because I only said I would 'try.' I didn't say I would definitely be there. I don't want to hear that word around here again. From now on, we either will do something or we will not do it, but we will not 'try' ... is that clear?"

Everyone nodded in agreement. "What you two are proposing is a band-aid solution for this problem." She looked at Joe and then at Frank. "We know this is becoming a frequent problem, and I think we have to make a plan as to how we are going to deal with it on an ongoing basis. We have to in order to restore our reputation."

She leaned back in her chair, signalling that she was finally done and someone else could have the floor. The men looked at her and then at each other for what seemed to them an eternity before Leigh spoke.

"I know how busy everyone here is, but I guess it is my department that is affected the most. My staff works hard to sell new air conditioners, furnaces, hot tubs, and so on, and we know that all our field staff is swamped with larger projects so we try ..." He looked at Betty and then quickly continued, "I mean we don't give people a firm date and hope the sales can be fitted in. Sometimes we lose sales, and sometimes we really peeve customers off if they have to wait too long, but we can't give them a definite time. I think we should have a full-time service man or two who do nothing but the installations and service work."

Frank slowly shook his head from side to side and responded, "There are two problems here. We need both someone who has a gas ticket and a plumbing ticket as well as someone who can do heating and air conditioning. I can't spare any of my guys, and I'm sure Bob has the same problem." He looked at Bob for support and saw him nod his head in agreement.

Joe spoke again. "I have an idea, but it will take a couple of days to investigate. Let's try to band-aid Mrs. Schultz's problem tomorrow, and I will come back with a plan for our Friday management meeting."

"Okay," said Betty. "But let's make this a priority. I don't want to be ambushed like this again."

They all agreed, and almost in one movement of chairs and people, the office cleared. On the way back to the shop, Bob looked at Frank and smiled in a way that sent the unspoken message that they had dodged another bullet. Frank just shook his head in unspoken agreement.

The next day passed quickly as Joe and an apprentice worked on the job for Mrs. Schultz. At lunch Joe reviewed with the young man everything that he had left to do and then left him to finish as he hurried off to his meeting.

The rest of the week seemed to pass all too quickly, and as it drew to a close, the managers gathered in Joe's office for their weekly project reviews.

As everyone settled down, Joe spoke. "I have given a lot of thought as to how to solve our service problem, and I think I have a possible solution."

"You're going to work nights?" Leigh said with a grin. Everyone smiled.

"Better than that." Joe acknowledged Leigh's humour and then continued on. "A couple of weeks ago I dropped in on a coffee shop bull session just as Dennis from Mountain Plumbing was complaining about how difficult business is and how some days he would just like to work for someone else."

"No one is going to hire that old fuddy duddy," Frank said. "He is too old and slow, and his number-one man, Leonard, isn't much better. I think the two of them installed the plumbing in the ark." He chuckled, and Bob joined in.

"Just a minute," Joe said earnestly. "I worked with those guys back in the mill years ago, and while they are not as young as you guys, they are only in their mid-fifties and they have a ton of knowledge and lots of years left. I think they could be our service department." Joe looked at the others for a reaction.

"Be serious, Joe." Betty jumped in first. "They are nice guys, but their company is always just one cheque away from being broke. You have said that yourself. How will they make money for us if they can't make money for themselves?"

"Because we have you." Joe looked at her and then smiled. "Think about it. Everyone likes Dennis and Leonard, but we all know they work too cheap and they give too much time away. They are good tradesmen but not good businessmen. If they worked for us and let us do the billing and collecting, I think they could make just as much money as they do now with less stress, and they would be great on service."

"They are good guys," Leigh joined in. "But do you really think we have enough work to keep them busy?"

"It doesn't take much to keep them busy," Frank added.

"Listen, guys, I think they are in a different place than you are," Joe interjected. "They don't want the constant rush and stress of new construction, and they don't want the stress of running their own business. With the work they have now and what we have to offer them, I think they could have steady work and not only would be happy doing it but would be good ambassadors for the company."

"Have you talked to them about this?" Betty asked.

"No. I wanted to run it by all of you first. What do you think?" Joe looked at Frank first.

"I don't really know the guys," Frank observed. "It's just that I know that they often quote an hourly rate considerably lower than ours and they still don't get much work, so it makes me ask why."

It was Bob's turn to speak. "I did a couple of small jobs with them before Joe convinced me to work here full-time. Joe is right—they are good guys, and everyone seems to speak kindly of them. But they do give away a lot of their time to people just to be nice."

"What do you mean?" Frank said.

"On a home renovation job for the bank manager, they came back a number of times to move lines because the wife couldn't decide where the washer and dryer should go. They never billed extra, saying they weren't busy anyway. I believe in keeping the customer happy, but she was the one who kept changing her mind. That banker had a lot more money than those boys, so why were they being charitable to her?"

"Because that is who they are," Joe said. "I think if they worked for us and let us handle the business end, we would all be better off."

"What have we got to lose?" Betty asked. "Go ahead and talk to them."

Joe was right. The two older plumbers did not like the business end of being in business, but had been forced into business just as Joe had been when the mill closed. Each year they made less than they had as mill employees, but they felt that they had no other option but to continue. They had no interest in the pains of growing the business and did not like new construction. They had found a niche in servicing several smaller businesses in town and doing the odd small service job. They occasionally competed with Joe for these types of smaller jobs, and they always undervalued their labour, so they found work but did not present a stumbling block to Joe's growth. Businesses that required large ongoing maintenance, such as the resort, did not consider them a professional or viable alternative. Joe and the two men had worked together at one time and still maintained respect and a loose friendship.

Joe met with Dennis and Leonard early the following week and was surprised at how quickly negotiations went. Joe offered to buy their inventory and equipment plus pay a small amount for their business number, and they agreed to join Joe, creating an independent service department focused only on service. They would receive a competitive wage and share in a profit bonus based on their portion of the business.

The two men plugged away at a steady pace and not only cleaned up the backlog of warranty items quicker than Frank thought they would but performed service and repair work for their former customers and took care of several larger service contracts Leigh brought in. The department grew by two apprentices that Dennis recruited, and in just over a year they became a significant profit centre.

Joe's Plumbing and Heating continued growing, but despite having good managers, Joe often spent sixty to seventy hours a week reviewing estimates, dealing with financial problems, checking on crews, meeting with clients, and solving a never-ending stream of other challenges.

"Yes," Joe said to himself as he soaked in the spring sunlight warming the deck, "the business is doing well, but is it really worth the price?"

Joe's frown eased, and a small smile broke on his lips as he thought back to some of the other problems he had faced that had, at the time, seemed so fatal to his business. He had held on and overcome them. He remembered the particularly tough times in the first few years when he seemed to be constantly on the verge of bankruptcy.

Joe reflected on the stress he and Betty had experienced when they thought they were going to lose the house after a large customer had gone broke still owing them a substantial sum of money. He remembered how depressed he had become and how Betty's faith in him and her hard work had helped them work through it.

Another time, an out-of-town general contractor brought a plumbing and heating company into town to work on his project and managed to win away a couple of large regular housing clients that had been with Joe for some time.

Again they persevered, and Betty not only worked hard at the business but lobbied the wives of the other local contractors to keep dealing with Joe's. Then one day, one of the previous clients was in a jam and needed someone to service one of their homes that had a toilet backing up. There were no local plumbers from the other company to fix the problem, so the contractor called the office and sheepishly asked Betty if she could get someone over to the house. Betty said they would be happy to do so and then added, "We will do anything to earn all your business back."

A week later the contractor dropped two house plans off and never used the other company again. With even less local work, the out-of-town company provided even less service to the remaining contractor, and he too was soon back dealing with Joe's. Joe smiled, remembering how embarrassed the first contractor was when he met Joe after that incident and how loyal a client he became when Joe just shrugged it off and welcomed him back.

Then Joe's smile faded as his mind returned to the problem at hand. This was definitely the most difficult challenge he had faced. Betty often expressed her feelings bluntly, like the time of the service problem. Sometimes she did annoy the guys, as they thought she should stay in the accounting office and let them handle the field problems. They had always been able to work through it in the past; this time it was different.

"How can I fire my wife and still maintain a good marriage?" Joe muttered the words out loud and thought how devastated Betty would be. Life would not be easy. He recalled the old adage "happy wife, happy life," and the knot in the pit of his stomach got tighter.

Joe was the official sole owner of the business, but he considered Betty an equal partner as she had worked countless days and evenings and consented to risking their assets for the sake of the business. He especially liked her ability to collect the outstanding bills; she was straightforward, tough-minded, and assertive, so she didn't mind asking for money, a part of the job Joe didn't like.

Betty's hard work and determination had been as instrumental to their success as his had been. She still managed the office and supervised a full-time bookkeeper, a receptionist/dispatcher, and any other employee she thought was in need of some direction. She had learned a great deal about the plumbing and heating business over the years and was not intimidated by some of the young tradesmen who tested her, thinking that because she was a woman they could put something over on her. Betty did not mince words and was quick to put them in their place. Her number-one priority was for Joe's to provide outstanding service, and she did not accept excuses for providing less than what she would want herself.

It was Betty's aggressiveness and the way she spoke her mind that had created tension between her and the managers. The breaking point had come yesterday, culminating in Bob, Frank, and Leigh taking Joe aside and stating that either Betty had to leave the company or they would.

Joe had been out at the old mill in the morning with a local group that was considering buying it, updating it, and putting it back into production. The thought of what it would do for the town and the added potential work was exciting to Joe, so he had purposely turned his phone off for the morning so as not to be distracted.

While he was at the meeting, one of Frank's apprentices had fallen off a ladder and broken his arm. He was taken to the hospital and treated right away, and although he was not seriously hurt, he would be off work for a while, adding more pressure to the schedule.

When Betty heard about the accident, she called all four managers into her office and began lecturing them on safety regulations. It had turned out the young fellow was using too short a ladder so he was overextending himself and was working alone at the time. Betty was upset and asked what would have happened if the injuries had been more serious.

"Not only could we have lost a fine young man, but our compensation rates would have skyrocketed and one or more of us could be charged," she was reported to have told them. Then she added, "You know safety is one of our key concerns. I don't think you guys are giving it enough consideration. I want to know how we intend to ensure this does not happen again!" With that, she had left.

The men told Joe later that Betty was way out of line. Not only were they very safety conscious, but their track record showed it. This was the first lost day due to an accident in over a year, and they routinely talked to the men about safety. This young fellow was gung-ho and wanted to finish his job before lunch, so he grabbed the closest ladder and was performing the work without thinking. "Remember when we were twenty-five?" Frank had said, "We thought we were ten feet tall and bullet-proof as well. This young fellow just learned in a most unforgettable way that he isn't."

With that, they told Joe they didn't know what else they could do to make Betty happy.

"We already have a safety officer checking on the sites and equipment. We hold regular safety meetings and put up all the compensation board posters, but we can't be holding their hands every minute of the day," Bob had commented, and the rest nodded in agreement.

"It is not so much that Betty had a right to be concerned; it is the way she always goes to the attack rather than discussing issues with us," Leigh suggested. "There are too many of these attacks, and everyone walks around like the floor is made of eggshells. We don't want the stress anymore. We are sorry. We know that Betty used to do a great job, but we are not sure why you even need her around the office anymore."

Joe didn't know what to say. He felt cornered and could not see a clear way out. He tried to reason with the managers, but to no avail. He asked for some time to think about a solution. Joe knew that if he approached Betty, she would confront the managers directly, making things even more difficult.

For the first time in all these years of business, Joe felt alone in deciding what he should do. He just wanted to run away and, in fact, had done just that. He came to the Lakeview Resort, supposedly to look at a renovation job, but the truth was that he just wanted to spend some time sitting alone on the patio.

He found it most serene here, as his mind came back to the pines and he looked out over the quiet lake. This was a place where he could think about the problem without interruption.

Joe was deep in thought when a stranger settled down at the next table and attempted to strike up a conversation.

"Enjoying the morning? This is such a great view," he remarked in a warm low voice.

Joe was annoyed as he came back to the present and looked at the well-groomed fellow with the close-cropped white beard, yellow golf shirt, bone white pants, and a smile to match. The man looked to be in his early sixties with laugh lines around cool blue eyes.

"Yeah, it is great here." Joe's answer was as curt as he could allow himself to be. But the fellow had a gentle and pleasant manner and persisted. Soon he had Joe engaged in a conversation about the plumbing business. Joe felt an almost immediate sense of trust, and before he realized it, he had relayed his entire story to the stranger.

As Joe spoke, the old fellow sat silently, stroking his short white whiskers, until Joe finished his narrative. After some time had passed and the two sat in the warm silence, the stranger finally spoke.

"So you are afraid that if you don't get Betty out of the office, your managers will leave the company?" He paused, not really expecting the obvious answer. "You believe that if that happens, you will not be able to handle the extra work load and they could take a lot of your business with them and become your competition?"

"Yes," Joe said, still staring out at the lake.

"On the other hand, Betty will feel betrayed and hurt if you tell her they want her to leave since she is as much a part of the company as you are?"

"That about sums it up." Again Joe's gaze did not stray from the distant vista. He thought the stranger had summarized the problem so succinctly that it almost trivialized it.

"It sounds to me like you need a consultant or to least to be part of a mastermind group," the older man said quietly.

That snapped Joe's eyes free of the horizon, and they seemed to smoulder as he turned to the old man. "Sir, I don't mean to be rude, but I work very hard in my business, and I've been very successful over the years. I don't know what you know about business, but I resent someone telling me that I need someone else or a mastermind group—whatever that is—to tell me what to do."

Joe rose from his chair and slid it back against the wall. "I want to thank you for your time, but I must be going now." With that, Joe started to walk away.

In his same thoughtful tone, the old man said, "I wish you well with this dilemma. Just remember, the seed of your success lies in the heart of your weakness."

Joe felt anxious as he suddenly realized how much he had shared about his business with a stranger and how little he knew about him. That white-haired old man probably did not know the first thing about plumbing or running a company. He was probably just some tourist here on his three-week vacation from a large union job and didn't have the foggiest idea what it was like to be front and centre on the firing line.

"I bet he never had to make a payroll," Joe muttered to himself, upset for letting his guard down so easily with someone he had never met before.

Joe was still steaming two miles down the road and cursing the old man under his breath. Rocks shot out from the tires as he brought the pickup to a halt on the gravel shoulder.

Checking for traffic, he turned the truck around and headed back to the resort, loose gravel spitting out from his rear wheels as he accelerated. Joe was not sure if he should give the old man a piece of his mind or apologize for his rudeness, but it was the last comment the old fellow had made that piqued his interest.

Joe was nervous as he left the parking lot, rounded the building, and stepped up onto the patio. He didn't notice the small smile that crept across his face when he saw the old man still sitting in the sun. As much as he resented how much he had opened up to this stranger, he was also thankful for having a neutral person to talk to, someone without an agenda or judgment, someone who just listened. Joe opted for a quick apology for his abruptness. Then, without sitting, he asked what the man had meant by his last comment.

"Remember the old saying, 'Dance with the girl who brung ya'?" the old man said, smiling back at Joe.

Joe nodded, concluding that perhaps not all the pipes were connected in this kindly old gentleman's mind. He tried to smile again, but it was weak. Joe was too tired to run and too nervous to sit, so he just stood there looking down at the stranger.

"So if I understand you," Joe said and paused, "I should stand by Betty.

But how do I do that without it costing me all my managers?" Joe's eyes were not focused, and he was speaking more to himself than the old man. Then, as an afterthought, he continued, "And just what is a mastermind group anyway?"

The old man continued smiling and looked up at him. "Sit down. I will be happy tell you."

THE BANKER |||||||||||||||||

Brian Barker threw the papers down on his desk, loosened his red power tie a little, and then, putting his hands behind his head, leaned back in his comfortable high-backed leather office chair. He closed his eyes and ran a number of ideas through his mind

Joe's loan application looked sound, and it was his job to sell money for the bank, but he felt this was a bittersweet opportunity.

Brian and Joe were about the same age, although his balding head and extra weight tended make Brian look older than Joe. Brian had been Joe's banker since he and Betty first began the plumbing business.

In the beginning, Brian remembered how he enjoyed coaching and assisting Joe about finance and felt that Joe's success was in large part due to his mentoring. But over the past few years, Brian felt that life had become a little unfair.

After all, he thought, *I have more education than Joe, and I have worked hard over the years to earn my position as the local bank manager. Joe's account is a good one, but this plumber, who knew little about finance or business, makes more money than I do as the bank manager. On top of that,* he remembered, *I seldom see Joe anymore as most of the business dealings are with Betty, and she is difficult to deal with.*

Brian had never forgiven Betty for getting a mortgage from another source when they bought the old service station just because his rates were a couple of percentage points higher. After all, had he not offered them years of free advice? Besides, he had room to move if she would have negotiated with him instead of just accepting the other offer. She did the same thing again last year after he had proposed a retirement saving program to her; she opted for one with a local insurance company instead. All she had to do was stop in and talk to him; he could have matched anything anyone else had, but she just proceeded on without confiding in him. *That,* he thought, *was a fine way to treat him after all these years.*

Joe's Plumbing was now looking for more funds for its continued expansion. Although the paperwork looked reasonable, Brian was thinking of his conversation the previous evening with Leigh during their regular men's golf night. Leigh, a member of his foursome, had mentioned the ultimatum the managers were planning to give Joe today regarding Betty, and it gave Brian cause to smile.

Joe's financial plan was solid, but if there were a risk that all three of the managers would leave, that would put the bank at risk. This was reason enough to turn down the loan. He could not help but smile again at the thought. Joe's Plumbing had been a good enough client over the years, but he was just a plumber. Maybe it was time Joe and especially Betty were reminded just how important it is to have a good banker.

Brian liked Leigh and thought he should suggest that if the managers did leave Joe, they should consider starting a company of their own. If they used their homes as collateral, he could probably put together a loan large enough to get them started in business.

Brian was familiar with Joe's books, and he thought there was room in town for a profitable competitor. He could get his wife to silently put some money in, and they could take a piece of the action. He had always dreamed about owning a profitable business, but then he remembered that he only had ten years left until he could draw his pension and retire. He would have to be crazy to risk that, he thought.

Brian did not want to lose Joe's Plumbing as a client, but it would be sweet to see Joe and Betty squirm a little. The situation could result in the managers forming a new plumbing company, giving the bank another client, or force

Betty to leave the company, which would give him personal satisfaction. Either way, things would be better for him.

Brian sat up and looked at the paperwork again. Perhaps the best thing to do would be to sit on the application for a week or so and see what happened. This would remind Betty and Joe of how important it is to keep your banker involved, and the added pressure of not knowing if the expansion funds are available could even help force Joe to make a quicker decision between the managers and Betty.

Brian liked the small feeling of power he was now holding over Joe. If Joe complained about the time it was taking to secure the loan, Brian could always fall back on his old habit of blaming the head office.

With that, Brian scooped up the paperwork, put it back in a file folder, and placed it in the side drawer of his desk. Smiling, he straightened his tie again, picked up the phone, dialled a number, and listened to it ring twice.

"Hello, Joe's Plumbing and Heating," the voice answered sweetly.

"Is Leigh in?" Brian asked.

"Yes, just a minute please."

"Hello. Leigh here." Brian recognized Leigh's cheerful voice immediately.

"Leigh, it's Brian Barker. I was wondering if you wanted me to pick you up for an extra game of golf late Thursday afternoon." Brian hoped his voice would not betray him as he felt a little on edge, as though he were treading on thin ice.

"Brian, yeah, that would be great."

Brian felt the enthusiasm in Leigh's voice and added, "Great. I'll stop by the shop at 5:30. And I'll book a tee time and call you back to confirm." Brian thought that by Thursday Leigh should know what was going on, and that man did like to talk.

Within the hour, Brian had booked the time at the local golf course, called Leigh back to confirm the time, and was preparing to go to lunch with another client. As he stood up behind the big wooden desk, he paused, looking at the drawer that held the file, and wondered for a moment if he had allowed some bit of jealousy to creep into his mind. Brian thought of himself as a fair man and a good banker, but the thought of Joe squirming seemed to be pleasing him just a little more than it should.

He reminded himself that he had liked Joe as a client and did not really wish him any harm, but there was to be a good feeling inside knowing that life was not always easy for Joe. *After all,* he said to himself, *Joe was nobody when he came in for his first bank loan, and I helped him get started.*

Brian felt a jealous pang at the thought of Joe, just a plumber, making four times the money the bank was paying him. *Life just is not fair,* he thought. *So sometimes it feels good to see those enjoying a little more success slip a little.*

Brian was still feeling the self-pity at his lack of success as he took his suit jacket from the coat tree by the door and slipped it on, tugging at his tie again. He took a quick look around the tidy office and headed out the door.

A FISH STINKS FROM THE HEAD

Joe accepted the old man's offer to sit down again, but he continued to stare at him, wondering if he in fact had any wisdom or if he was just another person with nothing invested who was more than willing to tell anyone who would listen how to run his business.

Joe remembered how his banker, Brian, had helped him when he started the business so many years ago but then continued to offer his advice long after Joe had quit asking for it.

Joe was always eager to learn and had a number of mentors over the years. One of his favourite mentors was Ed, now retired but still a good friend, who had owned a welding business that originally fabricated speciality equipment for the mill. Ed had built his business into a successful fabrication shop and had always said that the reason he had survived the downturn after the mill closed was he had expanded into other industries. While the slowdown had hurt him a little, he survived when others who had "all their eggs in one basket," as Ed put it, did not.

Ed had coached Joe on his own expansions into the heating business and then the retail sales. He also encouraged him to expand into both the commercial and residential business. Joe had learned a lot from Ed, and most of it just for the cost of a cup of coffee. Not that Ed didn't offer to buy; it's just they liked to play a game for the tab, and somehow Ed always seemed to win. The win would make him laugh, turning up the corners of his eyes as though it was a real prize. Joe liked Ed and wished he were back from his extended holiday so he could run this latest problem by him.

He had also considered visiting his lawyer or accountant, as they too were more than willing to offer advice. But he thought this was not really a problem they were versed in, and they were always on the clock.

Joe had attended a number of seminars and also hired a business coach who offered regular meetings by phone. Joe used his services for a short time and was not really surprised to find that the coach had no real training and his only business experience had been in a failed multilevel marketing business that sold vitamins. *Not that that is a bad thing*, he thought, *But the guy had never made payroll or had to risk his home for his business.*

Boy, he thought, *if I had all the money I have paid consultants for bad advice …* He squashed the mind traffic and returned to the present.

"Okay," he said to the old man, still unsure if he should continue this discussion. "So if firing the wife isn't a good idea, but I don't want to lose my key employees, what would a good consultant or mastermind group tell me to do?"

"Nothing," the old man stated flatly, and Joe could feel the hairs begin to rise on the back of his neck.

"Nothing?"

The old man straightened a little in his chair, and then, as he leaned forward, the tone of his voice became more serious.

"A good consultant or mastermind group doesn't tell you what to do." He paused and looked at Joe while the sentence sunk in. He then continued, "A mastermind group is a collection of like-minded businesspeople who, like a good consultant, share experiences and suggest alternatives. Ultimately each member is responsible for his or her own decisions." Joe's expression did not seem to change. He was listening and inside the wheels were turning, but his face did not betray his thoughts.

The old man explained. "The best situation is a mastermind group, headed by a consultant so that one member does not derail or distract the rest of the group. But whatever the final decision is, the group then supports each other because—who really knows what will work?" Again, the old man paused and then leaned back in his chair again and smiled as he continued.

"One of my favorite examples was the highly paid Decca record executive who was an expert in popular music. He sent out a rejection note that said, 'We don't like the sound, and guitar music is on the way out.'

"What if, in 1962, when Decca sent that rejection, the four young men believed this industry expert and gave up their dream of becoming the Beatles?

"No one has the right to impose his ideas on you; we can only offer each other suggestions and alternatives, act as a sounding board, and give support no matter what you decide." Again the old man smiled and relaxed back into the chair. He seemed to have all the time in the world and gave Joe the time he needed to process the information before leaning forward again, signalling that he wanted to continue.

Even Joe had to smile at the thought of all the regret the record executive must have felt over the years. Then as the old man leaned forward his thoughts quickly returned to the subject at hand.

The old man continued, explaining, "A mastermind group can have several members, but it operates on what a friend of mine calls the Law of Two, which states: 'Whenever two people bring knowledge and effort together for the attainment of a purpose, they create the power of a third, invisible, intangible mind. If a strong spirit of harmony exists between the two, they will begin to acquire expanded knowledge and new ideas from the invisible third mind they create.' Belonging to such a group will support and propel your business success."

The old man took a sip from his cup and then tilted his head back and closed his eyes to let the warm sun fall on his tanned face.

Joe stared at him; his mind seemed to have two streams of thought. One stream was thinking, *Is this guy real or is he a fruitcake?* The other processed what the old man had just said. After what seemed like a long period of silence but was in fact only a few seconds, Joe spoke, "I haven't even heard of these mastermind groups before. Where do I find one?"

"You form one." The man opened his eyes, straightened a little, and looked at Joe.

"When I started my first mastermind group, I got a manual from my friend's business, Max-U. I can get you an address, and if you like, they can even facilitate the group for you. The manual has a great format to keep the monthly meetings on track. You then find like-minded individuals you like and trust. I am sure you know some folks like that."

Joe thought for a moment and then said, "There is an electrical company that works on a lot of the same projects we do. We are not close friends, but I know the owner, and he seems to run a good shop."

"Excellent. Who else?"

"There are a couple of home builders I get along well with. I wonder if they would be interested."

"A few thoughts: First, if you want everyone to be open and honest, don't bring two competitors into the group, and while customers and suppliers can offer good industry insight and it can help build rapport, remember that you will be asked to share information you may not want them to know. A third thought is don't limit yourself to trades with a business similar to yours. Sometimes someone from the outside or another industry can offer a clearer perspective, like your friend Ed."

"Okay, I think I see what you mean. Too bad Ed retired and is rarely here anymore. I can't think of anyone else right now." Joe was running all the other business owners he knew through his mind.

"Have you met the new manager of this resort?" the old man offered.

"No, I heard he isn't beginning work here until next week. I plan to meet him as soon as possible, but this resort is a great customer of ours and you said that having a client in the group could be risky."

The old man smiled. "I have met him, and I suggested that he do the same thing when he takes over. He is a bright young fellow and has an MBA from a well-respected university. I think you might like him."

"I don't think he would be good fit for my group. You say he has an MBA, and I'm just a dumb plumber struggling with a mutiny."

"First of all, watch your language!" The old man's eyes narrowed and seemed to turn a steely grey. For the first time since they met, the gentleman seemed on the verge of being irritated. His voice and mannerisms seemed to turn the conversation into a stern lecture. "Your subconscious mind may begin to believe you, and it will respond in kind. There is nothing dumb about a man who starts and builds a successful business." Joe felt uncomfortable as the old man continued to look him right in the eye.

"The new manager may have more formal education than you do, but I am confident that there are a lot of things you could teach him about business—things you only learn from the experience of being on the front lines. Experience that comes not just from running a successful business but from founding and building one. Do you understand?" The old man continued to look Joe right in the eye as he waited for a response.

Joe felt embarrassed. He had taken a number of self-improvement programs and knew that good positive self-talk and attitude were a big part for his success, but he always felt a little uncomfortable around people with a lot more education. That was one of the things that made him feel uncomfortable around his banker, Brian. When he and Brian talked, it was more like sitting through a school lesson than having a conversation, and Joe never really liked school as a youngster. Then, almost as if the old man were reading his mind, the old guy's expression seemed to lighten a little as he continued.

"Mark Twain said, 'You should never let schooling get in the way of your education.' He also made a comment that we should be thankful for those who quit school at grade eight and start businesses so the university graduates have somewhere to work."

Again, the old man quit speaking for a moment and studied Joe's face. Joe let the words of Mark Twain ease his face, letting the corners of his mouth turn up at the thought. Joe wasn't sure what to say, but before he could organize a response, the old man continued.

"I always encourage education, but education and schooling are not necessarily the same thing. I would be willing to say you already have a 'street-smart MBA' in running a plumbing business."

Joe waited to see if the old man was done before speaking. "What about the fact that this resort is one of our biggest accounts? As you said, I don't think I want my clients to know my problems or necessarily my successes."

"Do you treat this resort fairly?" The old man's eyes narrowed, punctuating the question.

"Of course. We prize this account and give them the best possible prices and service. I would hate to lose this account. Still, we make money here, but I don't know that I would feel comfortable if the manager knew how much."

"Listen, the purpose of a business is first to get a customer and second to keep a customer. The outcome of doing these two things well is making a profit. Without a profit, you will not be around to continue offering the good service. No one respects or understands that better than an MBA. Can you agree with that?"

Joe nodded but didn't say anything as the old man continued.

"If the new manager sees that you have competitive pricing and still make money, he will respect and admire that. I guarantee it. Besides, if he is on your team and you are successful, which obviously you are, he will feel a part of that success. Just don't write him off until you have a chance to get to know him. I am sure that if you do work together, you will become close friends, as many mastermind partners do."

"If it works, I can see how it might cement our business relationship," Joe spoke, but more to himself than the old man.

"As I said, not all customers or suppliers are good people to have as part of your group, and I don't want to tell you what to do. But at least consider him." The old fellow looked at Joe and, relaxing again, released one of his friendly easy smiles.

"I will, but in the meantime, the problem I'm facing right now is immediate, and I have to deal with it in the next day or so. Do you have any advice on what I should do now?"

"Yes, but I'm not sure you are ready for it." Joe snapped back to present thoughts at the comment but didn't interject.

"Regardless of what the problem appears to be between your wife and the managers, from what you have said, I think you are simply experiencing an attitude problem."

Joe frowned as he took in the comment and said, "I understand all about how attitude controls action and actions determine results, but I think this problem is more than just a bad attitude between Betty and the managers."

The old man paused. "When there is poor attitude in a company, who do you think is responsible?" His steel eyes focused on Joe, letting him know that the lesson was not over and that it was clear that he would not proceed until Joe answered.

"People are responsible for their own attitudes, but it only takes one bad apple to disrupt an entire organization," Joe replied.

"A fish stinks from the head," the old man stated quietly. "That is one of the secrets of life." Then he leaned back, waiting for Joe's reaction. Joe turned the phrase over in his mind a couple of times before asking, "Exactly what are you trying to say?" The comment was still ringing in Joe's ears, as he could only see it as a comment on his own leadership.

"Attitude is a reflection of leadership," the old man said, and then he added, "It can be a bitter pill to swallow, but the responsibility of attitude lies completely with the leader. People are always eager to accept credit when a company has a good attitude, but no leader wants to believe that a bad attitude is a reflection of his own leadership."

Joe straightened, and then leaning forward he said in a strong, disapproving voice, "I don't think I agree with that."

"Good!" the old man interrupted.

"Good?" The comment caught Joe off-guard. "Are you wanting a discussion or a damn argument?" Joe's voice was beginning to rise a little. He did not like conflict at the best of times, and he certainly did not want to argue with someone he hardly knew.

"When two people agree on everything, one of them isn't necessary." The old man's smile calmed the air. "We can both learn more by listening to each other's different points of view than we can by agreeing and patting each other on the back."

"I can do a lot of things, but I don't believe I can change how people think. Everyone chooses, or is at least is responsible for, their attitude." Joe's comments were firm and stated with an air of authority.

"True, but a good leader motivates people to make the right choice. If someone in an organization is causing problems and the leader does not deal with it, then doesn't it become a failure of the leader? In Sun Tzu's book, *The Art of War*, he suggests that war is a result of the failure of strategy. What strategy do you have to provide a good attitude within the company?"

"I don't have a strategy, but this all seems to bring us back to my problem of choosing to either fire my wife or lose Bob, Frank, and Leigh." Joe paused and then said, "I don't think telling them they have a bad attitude is going to solve the problem."

"You don't have to tell them—the problem is not with them." Again, the old man smiled and stroked his white beard. "As I said, the leader must take responsibility for the general attitude of the organization."

Joe stiffened as the comments registered. His complexion turned a little redder. "Are you saying that I don't have a good attitude? I have a damn good attitude," he declared, his voice growing louder. "I think I'm a pretty positive guy, and I resent being told that I have an attitude problem. In fact, other than this problem, I think my people have pretty good attitudes as well." He leaned forward and started coming out of his seat.

Why am I wasting his time with this old fellow, he wondered. *Perhaps I should get up and leave.* But instead Joe slumped back down in the chair. He did not have any more to say. He was feeling tired, frustrated, and confused as to what to do next.

The old man just looked at him, so finally Joe spoke up again, this time more gently. "I appreciate you offering me advice, but everyone offers advice on how I should run my business, including my barber. I think what we have is simply a personality conflict between the managers and Betty." Joe let the comment out almost as if it was his inner voice escaping rather than a comment.

"Don't take it personally." The old man said, using his kinder voice, "Most leaders have a good attitude plus the knowledge and skill to build their business. I'm sure your people have good attitudes most the time, but they are not demonstrating it, and how you react now will affect their attitudes in the future."

Joe listened and said, "It seems that no matter what I do, this is going to be a problem." He was beginning to feel like there was no way out of this situation.

The old man smiled again. "When companies are small, the owner can micromanage and control what goes on between employees. As the business grows and employee interaction starts to take place, interactions where the owner is no longer involved—that's when conflicts and problems increase. Would you agree with that?"

Joe nodded his head as he thought about how much better everyone seemed to get along when there were only a few employees and he had made most of the decisions.

"Why can some people lead in a seemingly effortless manner, while I feel as though I'm trying to herd chickens?" Joe let his inside voice escape.

This time they both chuckled and then became serious again as Joe continued, "How can I keep these three guys happy without asking my wife to leave the business?"

"If you agree that the problems between your wife and the managers are caused by a poor attitude, and if you agree that only you are responsible for that attitude, I will tell you what I believe a good consultant or mastermind partner would suggest as a possible solution. Is that fair?"

Joe was still not sure he agreed, but he did not know what else to do, so finally he said, "Okay, suppose I agree—then what?"

"I have a tee-off time soon." The old man winked. "Tell you what—I have five questions. If you report here with the answers at eight the day after tomorrow and buy us breakfast, I will share some ideas with you. Is that fair enough?"

"I don't know. The fellows seem to want a quick answer," Joe responded and then added, "What are the questions?"

"Go back to the office and tell the managers this is a big move and you need a week to come up with a solution that will work for everyone. By resetting the agenda, you will begin to take back some control over the negotiations."

"What if they refuse and say I have to stick to their original time schedule? I don't want to play games and risk losing them."

"You indicated that this may have been coming for some time, but the situation seemed sparked by a specific incident. It's my guess that they were operating with emotion in the moment without a strategy and have no real back-up plan.

"If that is true, they will give you the time. If they do have other plans, then they may insist that you stick to the timeline. You will know how strong your negotiating position is. Another of life's secrets is to know where you stand. Or as the great American philosopher, Clint Eastwood, said in *Dirty Harry*, 'A man has to know his limitations.'" The last comment was made with a poor impression of Clint, and the old man chuckled and then returned to his serious voice as he continued.

"After you get the extra time, ask each of them, including Betty, to answer the following questions. Collect the answers, and I will see you at breakfast."

"I will give it my best shot, but what are the questions?" Joe pulled a wrinkled coiled notebook from his shirt pocket, opened it, and pulling a pen from the pocket as well, wrote as the old man slowly dictated the following:

1. If you could change anything about each of the other managers, Betty included, what would it be?

2. How do you think each of the other managers will answer that same question about you?

31

3. What strengths do you think each of the other managers brings to the company?

4. What strengths do you think each manager believes they bring to the company?

5. What strengths do you bring to the company?

"I think I can tell you what each of them will say," Joe said as he wrote the last question down on his pocket notebook.

"I really don't care what you think," the old man responded, standing up and straightening his shoulders. For the first time Joe noticed that he had a look of power and authority. He stood taller than his five foot ten frame; he was straight and held his chin high.

"Just get their answers and meet me here for breakfast," the old man said, and with that he walked down the path, stopped for a moment to admire a flower, and then disappeared behind the spring blossoms.

Joe sat for a while, staring first down the trail after him and then at the questions, wondering if the old man knew something or if he was crazy.

The old gentleman's comments intrigued him, and despite his own former abruptness, Joe was beginning to like the old fellow.

He pocketed his notebook, stood, and headed back to his truck.

THE GOLF GAME ||||||||||||||

"How was your day, Brian?" Leigh asked, easily lifting his clubs into the back of Brian's truck. Leigh was strong and took pride in maintaining his physique and golfing with his wife. In his mid-thirties, Leigh was just recently married, and having no children, he had a lot of time for golfing and involvement in the local arts community. He loved being involved, and he loved the visual arts. He had tried his hand at oil painting, and two of his works still hung in the house. He had also taken some drawing classes, which he enjoyed as much for the social contact as his artistic skill development.

This and his charming smile helped him build a large network of friends and clients.

'Fine," Brian answered with the vague meaninglessness response most people use when replying to the question. Inside his head he was still formulating how to approach Leigh about the goings-on with Joe without seeming too curious.

The short drive to the golf course was filled with the same level of empty conversation about the good weather, an upcoming golf tournament, and what the opening of the old mill might do to local real estate prices.

Brian was thankful that it was a slow day on the course as he and Leigh were not asked to make up a foursome and instead set out on the first hole together. The game began as they usually did with talk on the first few holes about the summer, their families, and the game. Then as they waited on the fifth hole for the foursome ahead, Brian turned and finally said, "So, how is it going at work?"

"I don't know," Leigh replied. "You know we gave Joe the ultimatum to either get rid of Betty or we are all leaving."

"Yeah. What is he going to do?"

"That's the part I don't know. Joe asked for a week's time before he gives us an answer and then asked us to answer a bunch of questions about each other, but he was sort of vague about what we were doing it for."

"That sounds a little strange, doesn't it?" Brian said, and then continued, "Are you guys really prepared to leave if Betty doesn't?"

"I don't know, and I think the others feel hesitant, too. I really like my job and working for Joe; it's just getting more frustrating going to work every morning knowing that Betty might stick her nose into whatever we are working on."

The foursome they were following finally moved on, and Leigh cleaned his ball and walked over to tee it up.

He kept his eyes on the foursome to be sure they were out of range as he continued, "I don't know what we will do, but I can't see continuing to work with Betty."

"Have the three of you talked about starting your own company?" Brian was nervous bringing up the subject but tried to make the comment more matter-of-fact than a question.

Leigh laughed. "I don't know how we could raise the money it would require to start a company like Joe's Plumbing."

"Not so," Brian replied. "If you have a good business plan and some equity in your homes, you might be surprised how easy it is to form a new business."

Leigh didn't comment right away. He teed up and drove the ball straight down the middle just short of two hundred yards. He continued to watch it roll until it came to a complete stop and then turned as he mulled over Brian's remarks over in his mind. As he put his driver away and Brian walked over to tee up his ball, Leigh said, "Hopefully, Betty will leave and we won't have to go there. And I am not sure that my wife would be keen for us to re-mortgage our house. She wants to start a family soon, and that nesting instinct is starting to take over."

Brian's ball stopped about fifteen yards short of Leigh's, and as he walked over and slid his driver into his bag, he added, "Well, if you do have to go there and need a hand putting a plan together, let me know. I can connect you with some people at the bank who can help make it happen."

Brian did not bring up the subject again, nor did Leigh broach the topic. After finishing the eighteenth hole, they compared scores. They were quite competitive, so Leigh was happy to have beaten Brian by two strokes. Brian pretended to care, but his mind was elsewhere today. The two wandered into the lounge, where they replayed a couple of the holes over a drink. An hour later, Brian dropped Leigh off back at his office. They parted with a promise to get together again in a week or so for a rematch.

Brian felt a little disappointed that nothing had happened at Joe's yet and was deep in thought about what he had said to Leigh. He was surprised that Leigh seemed to be reluctant to discuss opening a competing business. He didn't think Leigh would feel that he had been too aggressive in the suggestions he had made or would say anything to Joe. Overall, Brian felt happy with the seeds he had planted in Leigh's mind.

Leigh thought about Brian's comment and what it would be like to own a part of a business. In order to pull that off, he would need the other two men as well, and while Betty was aggressive and bossy, he wasn't sure he wanted to be a partner with the others either.

Up until now he had gone along with the others because Betty could be a pain, but now as he thought about his options, he wasn't sure what he would do if Betty did not leave the business. He thought he would finish Joe's silly questions—he owed him that much—and then set up a meeting with the others.

After a nice dinner with his wife, Leigh excused himself to finish answering the questions. He was beginning to think that he and the other two managers had made their demand without much forethought as to what their next move would be if Joe refused. In sales he had learned to always have a strategy, but now he realized that he was in the middle of a big deal without one. They had all allowed their emotions to take control, and things had been said in the heat of the moment without much thought as to where they might lead.

At the time, Leigh had thought Joe would just convince Betty to set up an office at the house and drop into the business a couple times a week to oversee the bookkeeping. He thought she would welcome the escape from the daily grind, but now he didn't know what would happen if Joe and Betty refused to have Betty step back.

What would the others do then? What would he do? For the most part, Leigh loved working for Joe's Plumbing and Heating and didn't know where else in town he could get a similar job. For all Betty's shortcomings, at least you knew where you stood with her. He wasn't sure he could go into a partnership with the others even if money weren't an issue. As much as he liked the other guys, they too had challenging behaviours and too often stewed about things rather than laying them out on the table. He liked to talk, and although he understood the frustration the others seemed to have in dealing with Betty and her directness, until the others started complaining, he really didn't let it bother him. In the end, he wasn't sure which was a more frustrating behaviour to deal with, the directness or not knowing how the others were feeling.

He cursed at the predicament he was in. He didn't want to lose his job, but he didn't know how to back down either. Sometimes he went along too easily because he just wanted to be liked by others. Sometimes he trusted people too much, and now his trust in his peers may have backed him into a corner. He didn't think any of them had given this enough thought.

Leigh would have liked to talk about the questions before answering them, but Joe was pretty insistent that all the questions be done by morning. He wondered what the others would say about him.

THE QUESTIONS ||||||||||||

"Joe, what the hell is going on? The staff is whispering all the time, and this afternoon I heard that there's some sort of ultimatum." Betty's eyes were cold as she greeted him at the door. She was holding a wooden spoon more like a weapon than the stirring implement it was. She turned on a heel, and all five foot five of her marched back the few paces into the kitchen and then briskly turned back to the stir-fry she was preparing.

Joe closed the door, saying, "Just a minute. Let me take my jacket off."

He hung it in the hall and followed Betty into the kitchen, where he tried to place his hands on her shoulders. She shrugged them off and turned to face him, her brown eyes now moist.

In all the years they had been married, there had only been a couple of times when they had exchanged angry words. Joe was a little taken aback as this was the most direct and angry he could remember seeing her. He spoke slowly and softly, not wanting to heighten Betty's emotions any more than they already appeared to be.

"I … I mean we have a problem with the department managers. It concerns you, and I am trying to work out a way to keep everyone happy."

"What sort of problem?" Her voice was quieter now but no less firm.

"First you have been a little distant with me the last couple of days, and then you give us all these silly questions, saying you are looking at a way to improve our communication, and then I hear that there is a mutiny brewing and I seem to be the only one who doesn't know what is going on." This was the closest to tears Joe had seen in Betty in some time. When it came to business, she was like a rock, but now she seemed out of sorts.

"As your partner, don't I have a right to know?" She looked directly at Joe, making him uneasy.

"I apologize. I should have told you right away, but I did not want to upset you before I had time to work out a suitable solution in my mind."

"Upset me? Don't you think being the last to know is upsetting? Now just what is going on?" Betty's voice was becoming sharper and louder.

"Betty, I think there is some sort of personality clash between you and the guys. You are so strong and outspoken; I think it might be intimidating them. I have met a fellow who is helping me with a solution." Joe was nervous about saying too much, but he also had never held anything back from Betty before.

"So what do they say is the problem? If they have a problem with me, they should address it with me, not go running to you. I think we should call them into my office in the morning and I should talk to them."

"Betty, they say they cannot work with you. They say they are going to quit, and if you call them in, I think they will." Joe sighed.

"Then let them quit! Joe, this is our company, and we did not spend all these hard years building this business so the employees can tell us how to run it. We ran the business before they worked here, and we can run it without them again if we have to." Betty's voice was getting louder but now was beginning to tremble slightly.

"Relax, Betty. Let's think about this before we do anything that can't be undone." Joe paused and took a deep breath to slow down the pace of their conversation. He watched Betty while doing so before continuing. "The company is a lot bigger now, and the fact is, we do need them." Betty looked at him, neither agreeing nor disagreeing.

"These guys are good employees, and for the most part, they do a good job." Again, he paused and looked to Betty for a cue.

She slowly shook her head in agreement but replied, "They were fairly good employees but I don't think what they are doing now is something good employees do, and I don't think we can afford to be held hostage by them.

Give in now and they will continue making more demands. It will be tough, but we can make it without them. Perhaps if you fire one, the others will change their mind."

"If they don't, who is going to oversee all the work and crews?" Joe took her hands and watched her as he waited for her answer. This time she did not pull away. They stood looking at each other for what seemed to be a few minutes, and then the sizzle of the pot reminded her that she had to keep stirring the vegetables.

She turned without saying anything, stirring for another minute and then, without looking at him, responded in a much calmer voice. "Joe, we have never kept secrets. We are partners, and I am most hurt because you did not trust to confide in me."

"I'm sorry, Betty."

She could tell he was, and she understood why. She had learned a long time ago that Joe avoided confrontation as much as he could, considering that he was in the construction business. He tended to bottle things up and keep them to himself, but this time she hadn't even seen this coming and it upset her.

Still stirring the pot, she asked, "Okay, so what do these questions have to do with it? And who is this fellow you say you are working with?"

"I met this fellow out at the resort. He had been giving me some advice, and he does seem to be very experienced with this sort of thing."

"What makes you think he knows anything about our circumstances?" Betty demanded.

"He is being both direct with me and respectful, and I feel good about that."

"How did you meet him?" Betty asked. "And what is he going to do with these questions?"

"We just met at the resort and started talking. I don't know how he is going to use the questions. All I am asking is that everyone answer them and give me a chance to review the answers with this fellow. If we don't like his suggestions, we can still do it your way."

"How much is this fellow charging us for this mysterious process?" Betty didn't try to hide her disapproval.

"Well, actually, he isn't charging us at all." Joe had already anticipated the next question, which he knew he could not answer.

"Why is this fellow offering to help you for free? Sounds to me like you are letting some interfering know-it-all tell us how to run our business. If he was any good, wouldn't he be charging us?"

"I don't know. We just met at the resort and sort of became friends. I can't explain, but I trust him. So let's just answer the questions and see if he can help, okay?"

It took a few more minutes of tense discussion. As they set the table together, Betty reminded Joe that she didn't appreciate him talking about their problems with strangers and not discussing them with her first.

Finally, the meal was ready and Joe asked where the girls were.

"They are still at school practising for a play. They will be home in an hour or so. I told them we would save something for them to eat, but you know them, they are probably eating junk food with their friends."

Betty seemed to calm down as they ate together. After they cleared away the dishes, Joe laid out a copied sheet of paper he had with the old man's questions. She read them over then began to answer them. He continued to tidy up the kitchen.

Joe understood why Betty was upset but wasn't sure how he could have handled it better. Later, the girls came in all excited about the play. They ate some of the supper that had been left for them then sat down and watched TV. Betty read the paper, and Joe reclined in his big leather chair, closed his eyes so as not to be disturbed, and replayed the events of the past few days in his mind. Betty's question kept coming back to haunt him: Who was the old guy, and why was he doing this?

Joe had a surprisingly good sleep. He rose early and made omelettes for the girls while Betty was still getting dressed. She came in and had her usual cup of coffee and a fruit dish. She said little but appeared to be in a much better mood.

"I brought a deposit home last night because I didn't have time to get to the bank yesterday," she said to Joe between sips. "I plan to stop in to the accountant's office and then do the deposit and go for lunch with Janet." Janet was a longtime friend, and they often turned to each other for support. Joe guessed this was partially an excuse for her to not go into the office today, and he was relieved.

Joe picked up the file with the answers Betty had prepared, gave her a quick kiss and the usual hug, and left for the office. Frank and Bob were busy in their offices, getting crews out for the day. When Joe asked if they had the answers for him, they each gave him a handful of papers and carried on.

Dennis and Leonard were just about to leave as Joe walked by. They had a minor crisis going on with a sewer backup. Joe felt happy that Dennis and Leonard were not part of the mutiny, although he was sure they knew what was going on. He thought it was because they were happy to have Betty doing the hard work neither of them had liked when they were running their own business. For the most part, they just steadily did their own thing, and everyone else seemed to let them be.

Joe looked in on Leigh and asked if he had his answers. Leigh had several sheets together and neatly stapled at the corner.

"This was hard." He smiled and then began talking about the questions and how much he wanted to write about each one. Joe thanked him and said he would review them with him in detail later but he had an appointment and had to run.

Like the first morning Joe met the old man, the warmth of the sun reflected off the white stucco as he stepped onto the patio at the resort. He was anxious to hear what the gentleman had to say, so he was happy to see him already sitting there.

"Good morning," said Joe, pulling out a chair and laying down his file folder on the metal side table.

"Isn't it a great morning?" The old man swept his hand toward the lake. Joe followed the gesture and thought about how lucky he was to live here. The air was still this morning, and the sun reflected off the smooth lake surface like a giant mirror. The surface was broken in the distance by two canoes, each with a couple paddling along the shoreline. They would paddle for a while and then coast as they talked to each other. Their voices carried in the still air, but not enough that one could actually hear what they were saying.

In the foreground, the dew still hung on the flowers and a gardener was working in the flower beds that followed the path down to the beach. Joe took it all in, thinking how strange it was that we live in such a beautiful place but often don't take the time to really see it. Then turning back to the old man he said, "Yes, it is."

"So did the questions help you discover some reasons why your staff and wife do not get along?" the old man asked, looking down at the folder.

Joe opened it and laid four piles of paper on the table as the waiter arrived with a coffee pot.

"I only looked at them briefly, and to be honest, I'm not sure exactly what they prove other than they really do have personality conflicts."

Joe moved one pile in front of the others. "Bob is the first full-time person I hired. He is an old friend of mine and looks after all the heating and air conditioning." Joe began to leaf through the pages. "The two other guys think Bob is a really nice fellow. He is really thoughtful and brings stability to the company. If they were to change anything, they would have him be a little more outspoken.

"Betty, on the other hand, sees him as too quiet and resistant to new ideas. She feels that he speaks and thinks too slowly. The only thing she thinks he brings to the company is loyalty, but she added that maybe he only stays because he's afraid of change."

"Do you agree?" the old man asked.

Joe nodded and said, "That pretty much describes Bob," to which the old man replied, "Green," and made a note on a piece of paper lying beside him. Seeing the quizzical look on Joe's face, he said, "I'll explain later. Carry on."

Joe moved to the next pile of papers. "Frank thinks Leigh, our sales manager, is too optimistic and talkative and should spend more time working on detail. Bob says he dresses too well for a plumbing shop but that he is good at sales. Both guys say Leigh is enjoyable to work with and brings a lot of humour to the workplace, although Frank thinks he should be a little more serious.

"Betty says he should be more serious as well and should clean up his van and do his paperwork better. She says she likes him more than the rest because he is more direct and has an outgoing personality. They all agree that he does know a lot of people and that helps us with sales."

"Yellow," the old man said.

Joe gave him that same quizzical look and then moved to the next pile without saying anything.

"Frank looks after the plumbing shop. Bob likes Frank and finds him very detailed and neat but comments that he worries too much. Leigh thinks that he should lighten up a little but also says that the estimates he prepares are so detailed and well done they are easy to sell.

"Betty says Frank drives her crazy. He is so picky, and everything has to be by the book; although, for her, rules are just guidelines," Joe added. "Betty thinks Frank could learn to bend or stretch a few rules in order to get things done quicker. The one thing she does like is that he doesn't spend a lot of time talking to the others."

"Blue," the old man said as he scribbled.

"Finally, Betty." Joe just looked at the last pile of papers before him. "I'm afraid this is where the problem is," he said, taking a deep breath before beginning.

"Bob thinks she changes her mind too often. She acts too quickly and demands too much. Frank says she doesn't pay enough attention to the details and makes decisions without having all the information. Leigh says she angers quickly, speaks curtly, and is too direct. They all feel she should stay in the office and look after the administration staff, but she is always telling the managers what to do and often doesn't know the technical details of the job. I think maybe they also resent being told what to do by a woman."

"I don't think being a woman is the problem," the old man said and then sipped his coffee before continuing. "I knew by the way you described her earlier that she would be Red."

The old man made a note and looked up and remarked, "I believe what you have is a communication problem caused by four core behaviour styles working together but not understanding each other."

"Understand each other? Sometimes it seems like they speak totally different languages," Joe said, letting his frustration show. "But how do I fix that?" he asked, slumping back into his chair. "And what are the colours all about?"

"Most psychologists agree that there are four basic dimensions of human behaviour that can be measured, and all our behaviours fall into these categories. These include how people react to problems, how they influence others to their point of view, how they view the pace of their environment, and how they follow rules and procedures set by others. It is referred to as DISC behavioural psychology. Have you heard about it?"

"I think I have, at a workshop. If I remember." He paused. "Some people were labelled as drivers, socialisers, and amiable, or analyzers, or something like that. We even did a quiz on the Internet where we had colour results. I think we decided that I was amiable," Joe said.

"Close; that is a very simplified version of it. Each person is not any one style but demonstrates each dimension to some greater or lesser degree.

"I have a friend who uses behavioural profiles to address your very problem. She prefers to use nonjudgmental or neutral descriptors to illustrate or describe the core styles. She calls it the 'language of colour,'" the old man said.

"I haven't heard about her. Is she from around here?" Joe asked.

"No, this woman works all over North America. The program I am talking about she calls the 'Chameleon Communicator.' She uses colour images and text as it has been proven to increase participation by 80 percent and memory retention by over 200 percent. In short, people really do learn, remember, and use course material taught her way."

"So how does that help me?" Joe asked, leaning into the back of his chair.

"If we review the last two questions you asked everyone, I think it will become clearer. Do you have the responses for them as well?"

"Yes, I asked each person the questions. I still don't see how that is going to solve the problem of the men wanting me to choose between my wife and them." Joe's voice trailed off.

"It will all become clear at our next meeting, but I have some things to tend to right now."

The old man looked down at his watch. "What about 4:30 this afternoon?" Then, without waiting for Joe to reply, he began moving briskly toward the patio door.

Joe stood with his mouth half open and watched him disappear inside. Joe turned and walked to his truck, even more frustrated than before.

I am beginning to think Betty is right. This guy is just interfering, and I must be the one who is nuts for allowing him to lead me on. Joe tried to squash the thought, but it kept coming back as he drove into town.

LEIGH AND THE BANKER |||||

Brian was still thinking about Leigh and his seeming reluctance to discuss forming a new company to compete with Joe. He thought he should bring it up again at their next meeting.

The more he thought about it, the better the idea seemed. He knew Joe was making good money—too good, he thought. He still resented the fact that Joe was making so much more than he did.

Sure, Joe was willing to donate to all the causes, but he never got too involved personally like he did. He always used the excuse that he was so busy with his business. *Like he is the only one with a stressful job,* Brian thought. Leigh would be a good PR guy for the new company; he always seemed to make time to get involved.

Brian recalled seeing Leigh at most of the gallery functions as well as being the host for the Christmas tree auction at the annual hospital fund-raiser. It wasn't only that Leigh was present at the events; he always seemed to be at the centre, as people really liked him and his personality seemed to shine in group settings.

After the first golf game, Brian had made a few phone calls and found a supplier of heating equipment that competed with the line Joe carried. The man was eager to have someone represent his product lines in the community.

Brian was sure he could put together the money and the products if only the guys would leave Joe and start their own company. He did not want to get caught pushing the idea too hard, and he was not sure if the thought of making some extra money was motivating him or just the thought of taking Joe down a peg or two. He smiled as he imagined how Betty would react once she heard that her management team was now their competition.

Brian thought he would risk one more call. Leigh picked up on the third ring.

"Hello."

"Hi, Leigh. I was just thinking you should give me a chance to beat you at a round of golf." Brian chuckled.

"Always up for a game," Leigh replied.

"Great. By the way, how are things going with you and the other guys? Did you mention what we talked about the other day?" Brian held his breath.

"Sorry," said Leigh. "What did we talk about?"

"You know, the three of you starting your own business. I just happened to notice that one of your suppliers' competitors is looking for someone here to represent them." Brian breathed again.

"Oh, I don't know. We don't know the first thing about setting up a business."

"Well, you know I'd be happy to help you. That is what I do," Brian said.

"That is really good of you, Brian, but there are lots of suppliers, and there is always one of them looking for someone to sell their products. I think Joe has the best lines tied up."

"Well, there is always room for healthy competition," Brian suggested. "So you never talked about it at all then?"

"We never got together again as a group, so no, I didn't get a chance to mention it to the others."

"Well, keep me in mind if you do. I'd be happy to give you a hand."

Brian thought Leigh was feeling uneasy talking about it so he changed the subject. "What about tomorrow, tee off at five?"

"I can't play tomorrow, but maybe after work the next day. Does that fit into your schedule?" Leigh said, his voice a little lighter.

"That would be great. Pick you up at five?" Brian was a little disappointed that the topic of a new business got dropped so quickly. *How could he light a fire under these guys? There is a great opportunity here and they just don't see it.*

"Hey, I'm not a banker." Leigh's voice cut through Brian's thoughts. "Remember—my day doesn't finish until five. Will six work for you?"

"Six is fine. See you then." Brian hated the old jokes about banker's hours. He put in some long and stressful days himself. Brian wondered if he should try to approach one of the other guys, but he did not have a connection with them like he did with Leigh. He thought they should like the idea of owning their own business, but he understood that most people are afraid of the risk. He let the thoughts dissipate as he looked up the number for another client to take to lunch.

RED IS FIRE ||||||||||||||||||||

"Hello," Joe said as he approached the old man sitting at what was now their regular table. He pulled out his chair and dropped the file on the table. The added stress of this situation was causing Joe to feel tired by midday. *There are so many more constructive things that I could be doing,* he thought.

"I hope the answers to these questions will tell me how to resolve this conflict. The guys didn't speak to Betty yesterday, and she spent a half hour ranting at me on why we should fire all three. I don't know if I can take another day of this." Joe's voice was strained and drained of any energy.

The old man looked Joe over and then picked up the file and began to thumb through the pages.

"Let's look at what each person said the other managers' strengths are and what strengths they think they bring to the company," the old man said as he began to look at each page a little slower and added, "Then we will look at what each thought the other members of the management group would change in them if they could. That will confirm my first suspicions about their behavioural style or colour."

Joe sat up a little straighter and said, "Betty said having a tough mind was her main strength," Joe began. "She sees the big picture and knows how to improve the bottom line. And I have to agree. We would never have made it this far if it wasn't for her."

The old man made a note but didn't say anything, so Joe continued.

"She says she will not be pushed around and that she is not afraid to correct the employees when necessary, collect money, or do whatever is required. She feels that the employees would change her to be softer or more easygoing if they could, but she has no interest in changing."

The old man made a check mark in his notes. "Red is for fire; these people can heat up quickly. Red is the colour people get when they are angry; it is the primary emotion for Reds. They are almost like a bull. When they see a red cape, they charge."

Joe shook his head in agreement and said, "That sounds like Betty." And he smiled for the first time all day.

"A high Red person likes to try new things; they like a fast pace and a challenge. They are results oriented and aggressive and can help a company to be competitive," the old man continued. "They don't feel they need other people around them and can intimidate others. Does that sound like Betty?"

"I'll say," Joe said.

"Good. Let's leave that for a moment. Who's next?"

"Leigh, our sales manager," Joe replied. "He brings an ability to relate to other people, but some people feel that he talks too much. If they could change something, it would be to make him quieter. One comment was that he is too optimistic." Joe looked up from the quick notes he had scribbled before the meeting.

"Yellow, the colour of sunshine. That is what Yellow people spread." Again, the old man made a check mark. "This style's main emotion is optimism. These folks can be very influential in promoting a company, and they love to socialize.

"People who have this as their primary style can be great promoters. They bring laughter and fun to the workplace and are willing to work through conflict. The Yellows like to be part of a team, and they like to be liked." He looked at Joe, wrote something in his notes, and then turned the page.

Joe looked at the next sheet of paper and began, "Bob feels he offers the company stability and is a good team player. He thinks the others might find him too conservative or slow to accept new ideas."

"Just as we thought, he is Green, calming, like the forest," the old man said. "This style resists change; they will offer counsel to others and bring steadiness to a company. The Green dislike confrontation and may not voice their opinion, especially if they feel challenged."

"Bob is like that. I really like him; I think he is really a nice guy," Joe said.

"Of course you do," said the old man and made another note. "Most people like those who are high Green. They make up 45 percent of the world, and my guess is that this is your style, too." He looked at Joe and smiled.

"No, I think I am better than that. I can be really tough when I want to be," Joe said defensively.

"It's not about being better. There is no better. This is not about being right, wrong, good, or bad," the old man assured him. "Each style has advantages and disadvantages. You are what you are, but once you know that, you can adapt for short periods of time. People like people like themselves, so if you can turn up the Red when talking to a Red or take the time to be more exact when talking to a Blue, they will like you better. If they like you, they will listen and be more willing and able to communicate with you."

"Blue?" Joe asked.

"Sorry, I am getting ahead of myself. Read me your notes on Frank."

"Frank, my plumbing manager. He feels he is very thorough and exact. He is careful not to make mistakes and does good work. He thinks the others do not work as hard as he does and feels that they would like him to lighten up and be friendlier." Joe looked up from his notes.

"Blue and cool like the ocean. The Blue style follows all the rules. They like formulas and structure. They prefer procedures to people. Some may see high Blue people as aloof. They are often found doing a good job at accounting, engineering, estimating, and so on. Their main emotion is fear, especially fear of making a mistake."

"That would be Frank," Joe said, a little amazed at the pinpoint summary of a man he'd come to know over more than a decade.

"So you were right about the colours you chose yesterday," Joe said. "But doesn't this confirm my suspicion that this is a personality conflict? Betty is just too aggressive for the guys, and they can't work with her. How does knowing this solve the problem?"

Joe was beginning to feel as though this had been a waste of time. It only proved what he already knew. They just can't work together. Then his inside voice escaped once again, "Why can't they all just be Green?"

"That would bring about a new set of problems. I am sure you agree with Kermit the Frog's lament, 'It ain't easy being green'?" The old man smiled.

"Joe, we are not measuring personality. We are measuring behaviour styles, and not only can the different colours, or styles, work together, but once they learn how, they will form a stronger team than one made up of only one or two styles. You may not see it now, but you are very lucky to have these people as your core management team."

"That just doesn't seem possible right now," Joe said.

"The problem is that we all think our style is the best style and everyone should be like us, but each style has something to offer the team. If each person learns to respect the other styles by modifying their own behaviour to be closer to the style of the people they are communicating with, they will find they will enjoy clearer and closer relationships. Does that make sense?"

Joe rubbed his chin. "It all sounds good, but how do I get them to buy in?"

"You can't. You need a specialist. The problem most of us businesspeople have is we think that because we have been so successful in the past, we know the best way to succeed going into the future." The old man looked at Joe for consensus before continuing.

"The truth is that most companies can buy the same raw materials and equipment as their competitors and turn out the same product, but the companies that really succeed do so because they have a superior team that keeps them ahead of their competition. Agreed?"

"Agreed," Joe said.

"No one has all the answers or can do all the jobs, so the best companies hire the best consultants to assist them in keeping in the forefront," the old man finished.

"Is that what the Chameleon Communicator lady you mentioned yesterday does?" Joe asked.

The old man laughed. "Yes, that is what she does and who I'd use, but she is in demand and can be hard to book. I can get in touch with her if you are interested."

"I am, or do you think she'd be too busy for us?" Joe asked.

"I can call her. She is part of a larger team that includes other qualified professional behavioural analysts as well, so if she is busy you could book one of them."

"If you say you like this lady, I'd like to ask her first. It sounds like she is good," Joe said.

"She is good and owns a company that has a number of very sophisticated assessment tools that form the core of their consulting practice. Among other things, she teaches people how to adjust their colour, meaning their behavioural style, in order to succeed."

"Sounds expensive," Joe said and paused. "Any idea what she charges?"

"What are your problems costing you now?" The old man looked at Joe and then added, "I believe that a good consultant shouldn't cost. If they cannot identify what your current problems are costing you and then show you how you will make much more money than their fees, you should not hire them." He sat back and looked around. They were still alone on the patio. He took in a breath of the warm evening air and then continued.

"If someone makes you more money than it costs, does it matter what they charge? I'd happily pay a consultant $100,000 if I was convinced that she would increase my profit by $1,000,000. Doesn't that make sense?"

"I suppose so," Joe said slowly. "But there must be a cost to begin with."

"I am not trying to sell her services, but how much will it cost you if all your managers quit? Or worse yet, if they force Betty out of the business?" The old man paused to let the words sink in and then said, "I am sure the one-day session would get your team all on the same page." The old man stroked his beard thoughtfully. "But I think you should talk to her about more than just the one session."

"Betty will have a coronary if I spend a lot of money. I think the Chameleon thing may be out of the question," Joe fretted.

The old man continued talking about how much more profitable the company could be if everyone communicated better. He ended his short speech by saying, "I actually don't know what she charges or if she would even do a small assignment like this. Normally she reviews the client company in more detail and then, in consultation with the management team, determines how much she can increase the bottom line over a longer period of time and several sessions. Then she works out a fee based on a small percentage of that amount."

"This sounds like a really big investment of time, too."

"It can be," agreed the old man. "But Rome wasn't built in a day, and changes to an organization take time to take hold."

"I suppose. I know that I certainly think differently now compared to when we started the business. And I charge more now, too." Joe grinned at the memories.

"I know she has even offered to run a complete program for companies at no charge and just take a percentage of the profit increase. As far as I know, everyone has turned that down, saying later that, by comparison, the fee they were charged was a bargain."

Neither of the men spoke for a few moments, and then the old man said, "How much more would you make if your bottom line went up an extra 2 or 3 percent?"

Joe didn't answer, but he smiled. The old man knew why.

"I would suggest that you can't afford *not* to hire her, but it doesn't cost anything to talk to her. If her fees are too much perhaps she can recommend someone less expensive."

"You're right. When I think of the cost of advertising, interviews, reference checks, training on our computer system, I get tired. The loss of just one manager will cost us $50,000 or more," Joe calculated.

"Who knows what other costs there might be or what the lost opportunity costs are?" the old man questioned.

"So where do I start?"

"I suggest you start by talking to Betty about what we discussed."

"This all sounds just a little too easy to me, but I'm willing to try anything right now," Joe said with a sigh, "How do I arrange to meet the Chameleon Communicator?"

THE NEXT STEP I||||||||||||

The three division managers met at the local donut shop Saturday morning. Leigh was the last to arrive and grabbed his usual coffee and a plain glazed donut before joining Frank and Bob in a booth near the rear of the shop.

Frank spoke first. "So how did you score on your test?" He chuckled.

Bob sipped his coffee then said, "I don't really understand where we are going with those questions. Do you?"

"I don't," Frank admitted. "I'm afraid Joe is trying to turn us against each other. What do you think, Leigh?"

Leigh swallowed his bite of donut. "Relax, Frank. I don't think there is anything sinister going on. I think Joe is just trying to see where we agree and where we see challenges." He picked up his coffee and took a loud sip.

"What about you?" Frank asked, turning his gaze toward Bob.

"I have to agree with Leigh. I think Joe is just grasping at ways he can keep both us and Betty working."

"Perhaps we jumped the gun and shouldn't have given Joe the ultimatum so quickly," Leigh said.

"I disagree," Frank replied. "We've been putting up with Betty for a long time, and things weren't going to change."

Leigh and Bob nodded in agreement.

Frank shook his head as he continued his rant. "She drives me crazy. She changes her mind on what she wants on a regular basis, she doesn't follow up, she gives you only half the information, and then she gets upset when you don't give her what she wants."

"But what if Joe doesn't agree to have Betty step down?" asked Bob.

"I can see that Joe is in an awkward position. I wouldn't want Betty mad at me, and I don't have to live with her!" Leigh sighed.

"I have known Joe a long time, and I don't know if I can follow up on our threat." The concern in Bob's voice was audible. "I can't afford to leave, but I would hate to go hat-in-hand begging for him to take me back."

"I feel the same way, but I work long and hard to create accurate estimates. I buy right and get material to the job site on time – yet Betty has no appreciation for that." Frank ended his rant with a long drink from his cup.

"Joe doesn't want us to quit any more than we want to. Didn't you see how relieved he was when we agreed to give him more time?" Leigh said. "He needs us as badly as we need him."

"I disagree," Bob responded. "He isn't going to choose us over Betty, and I can see her letting us go."

"Maybe we should think about starting our own shop," suggested Leigh, looking at the other two managers for a reaction.

"There is no way I can afford to go into business," Bob replied.

"I'd be interested, but I can't afford it either," Frank said and then added, "If we did, I would want a clear agreement on what everyone is going to do."

Leigh felt that the comment was directed specifically at him. Frank often made comments when Leigh took off early to go golfing or didn't come in first thing in the morning if he had been out late on a sales call the night before. Even with the banker he had been careful not to golf on company time, but had it been with the maintenance manager of a large company or the superintendent of a new construction company, Leigh considered a golf game to be part of his job. This was one of his concerns about being involved in a partnership. *But still,* Leigh thought, *this might be an opportunity.*

Leigh was good at schmoozing clients and he knew it, but Frank considered that to be a waste of time. "Just give them the facts and get their signature," was a comment he often made. Leigh was a little nervous that Frank did not see the value he brought to the company, and getting into a partnership with him might lead to more trouble than he had now.

"Confidentially," Leigh said, gazing pensively into his cup, "Brian, from the bank, told me he could get us funding and help us set up a business if we wanted to." Leigh looked at the others for their reaction before continuing.

"I'm not sure if I want to get into my own company right now, but I am prepared to explore it if you guys are."

Bob stirred his coffee and tapped the spoon on the side of the cup. "I like the security of working for someone else," he answered. "Owning part of a company sounds like a good idea, but I would need to discuss it with the wife. It seems a little risky to me, and I don't want to do anything that would put my house at risk."

"I think it's worth looking at the numbers before we decide," Frank suggested.

Leigh broke the moment of contemplation. "Let's see if Joe comes up with something new on Monday. In the meantime, I will call Brian the first of the week and see if we can meet with him later in the week."

Bob and Frank nodded their agreement. They all finished their coffee in an awkward silence and then left to go their separate ways.

As promised, Leigh called the banker on Monday, but Brian was out. When he returned to the bank, Brian saw the message and called Leigh. This time Leigh was out on business and couldn't be reached.

"Tell him his golf buddy, Brian, called to arrange another game," Brian told the receptionist. "He can reach me at home this evening." With that he hung up, wondering if something had changed at Joe's Plumbing and Heating.

MEET THE CHAMELEON |||||||

Joe and Betty seldom disagreed, but Joe was still reluctant to share with her the conversations he had been having with the old man. He was not sure she would like the idea of bringing in an outsider to work out their personnel problems, especially at the costs he thought might be involved.

Joe felt that if he did not package it right, Betty might take it as an insult and not buy into the idea at all. He had learned some time ago that if Betty felt someone was threatening or challenging her, she used the old adage that the best defence is a good offence.

In fact, that was a big part of the problem. If she became defensive toward the employees, she would turn up the heat. They, in turn, would become intimidated, withdraw, and resentfully let her have her way.

Unlike Betty, most of the employees tended to keep their feelings bottled up inside where they festered. This is what had led to the managers joining forces and delivering the ultimatum to Joe. If she would only show them, some of the side of her that he knew. Betty was really a caring person and loyal to a fault. He knew she was generous and donated her time and money to a number of community causes, but at the job she kept her tough business mask in place.

Joe had agreed with her belief that everyone is replaceable, and they had to replace the odd key person over the years, but he felt they could not afford to lose all of the managers at the same time.

Betty had to buy into the program or he was in for months of hard work trying to run the company himself.

After supper, the girls were doing the dishes and Joe told Betty that he wanted to drop by a potential new client's construction site just to have a look at where the services came in. He asked her if she would go with him and then they could also go out for a coffee after.

At first she declined, giving a number of reasons, but Joe confessed that he really wanted the two of them to be alone to go over a couple of things that were bothering him. That worked, and soon they were sitting in a booth at the local coffee shop.

The server set the coffee down, smiled, and walked away before either of them spoke.

"So what do you want to talk about?" Betty kept her eyes on Joe's face as she raised her cup and took a sip.

Joe began by telling her a little about the old man and relayed what he had learned about the different behaviour styles based on the questions they had all answered. He ended with a general statement that perhaps everyone in the office could benefit from having a retreat based on learning some new management and communication skills.

Betty continued to sip her coffee and listen until the last comment. "I don't think we have a communication problem. It seems to me that everyone did pretty much as they're told up to now. My concern is spending money on employees who may not stay with us for very long."

"That is my point, Betty. We should be helping build their skills up so that you and I don't have to be telling them what to do. I would like to have the time to travel and enjoy doing things together again instead of both of us working seven days a week."

"I don't think teaching them communication is the answer then," said Betty. "We need to find a way to motivate them so they are more competitive and work harder. It seems to me that Leigh communicates a little too much. He is always laughing and chatting it up while Bob and Frank take all day to decide where to have coffee. Until we find a way to light a fire under them, I don't know how we could leave them alone for very long."

They both took another sip of coffee, and then Joe spoke again. "Maybe we could find a way to have them motivate each other. The old man speaks very highly of this Chameleon Communicator lady, and I'd like to talk to her about her services."

"How much would that cost us?"

"I don't know. I talked to her on the phone briefly today, and she told me that the old man had called and asked her to get together with us as soon as possible. She said that he was a good friend so she could arrange to meet us fairly soon."

Betty thought for a minute and then said, "This sounds like it will be very expensive to me."

"I thought the same thing, and then I was reminded that our people are our most important asset, and we spend less on maintaining them than we do the vehicles they drive. The old man said there were other companies who offer programs for less money. Maybe I could shop around and try to find one of them." Joe knew that while Betty always considered the bottom line and worried about getting the best deal, she also preferred to have the best.

"I like to get the best deal, but if we are going to spend money, let's make sure we get the best," she said, playing into his hand just as Joe had predicted.

"Okay, then why don't you call her and see if you can get a deal? I will give you the contact information at the office later." Joe felt that if Betty did the negotiations, she would have more invested and therefore find more value in whatever they finally decided to do.

"Fine. If you really think it's necessary, I'll call her tomorrow," Betty agreed.

Joe sat back and actually tasted the coffee he'd been drinking.

The next afternoon Betty walked into Joe's office, closed the door, and said proudly, "I have negotiated a really good deal to review our entire needs, but to begin with we can start with a Chameleon Communicator program next week."

"Next week? The old man said she is really booked." Joe looked surprised.

"The lady said she was booked for the next three months, but I insisted that we needed the workshop right away, so after a couple of calls, she said one of her regular clients would move their date back so we can have this program next week." Joe loved the way Betty could get excited when she took on a project and the way she could get results.

"So how good a deal did you get?" Joe asked.

"Well, she asked if I would want someone teaching business skills to our people who couldn't even get paid her own regular rate. I could see her point, so I agreed we would pay her regular price."

"So is it expensive?" Joe asked, still not sure how much this was going to cost.

"She told me that her services should save or make us far more than what the costs. She then explained all the other services she provides to assist companies to grow and profit. I feel we should be looking at a more long-term assignment." Betty was fully engaged, and her excitement and energy had changed for the better already.

"Besides the first session, I think we should have her do an analysis of what services we may need and how much they should save us versus what the costs would be," Betty said, punctuating each point with her finger stabbing the air.

Then, more pensively, she commented, "I liked the lady. I really connected with her. I have good feelings about this."

"Good," Joe said. This time he kept his inside voice inside as he thought, *Hopefully, this lady is magic.*

Joe's next task was to get a commitment from the men not to take any further action until after the retreat. The next morning he took each of them aside to explain about the program as best he understood it.

Leigh seemed distant at first but agreed. Bob anxiously agreed to participate, and Frank said he would for Joe's sake but that he didn't see how it would change anything.

SHOWDOWN |||||||||||||||||||

When Brian called, Leigh explained that the other men were willing to sit down and listen to how a new business might be structured. They agreed to meet in the evening at Leigh's home. It was a small town, and they did not want to be seen in public making plans.

Leigh's wife had made up some tasty treats and brewed a pot of coffee and had gone out to meet with a couple of girlfriends for the evening.

Leigh had stocked the fridge with a case of cold beer. He looked around his home. Although not large, it was well decorated and very comfortable. Two love seats and matching leather couch formed three sides of a square with a large TV and stereo on a simple glass stand forming the fourth side.

On the wall opposite the TV hung two large original modern art paintings created by a well-known local artist. Two smaller landscape pieces depicting a local mountain scene hung on either side of the TV. One end of the room had a large picture window framed by light-coloured elegant drapes that popped out from the dark chocolate–painted wall. The other was divided from the dining area by a three-sided fireplace. To the side of the dining area was a bar that separated the dining area from the kitchen.

Leigh had turned on some low smooth jazz for background, placed napkins and treats on a large coffee table in the centre of the square, and took the liberty of setting out some school scribblers and pens in case the others wanted to take notes but didn't think to bring anything to write on.

The men arrived one by one, with Brian coming in last.

As he entered the room, Brian coyly mentioned that he hoped they would all come to a satisfactory agreement with Joe and there would be no need to strike out on their own. He then said that he really liked Joe and appreciated him as a bank customer, adding that he didn't want to appear to be helping start up a new competitor.

"On the other hand," he noted, "we too are in business, and I don't want to miss out on a new business start-up if you decide to go it on your own. After all, that is how most businesses start. Do any of you have any questions before we start?"

He looked at each of his long-time client's managers gathered in the room.

Bob said he wanted to be clear that he was mainly interested in the information right now and not sure he wanted to go into business.

Brian answered, "Of course. That is the only reason why I am here tonight." No one else spoke.

So Brian began. He explained the basic need for good professionals, including a good lawyer, an accountant, and a banker, and how each would advise them on the type of structure to set up. He briefly touched on the advantages of proprietorships, partnerships, and incorporations and the differences between them.

He then moved into funding a new company and gave them some books and brochures on how to write a business plan and create a budget. He touched on equipment, leasehold improvements, inventory, and what a lending institution would gladly lend and what they would find risky.

He ended with how each of them could each re-mortgage their homes to take out equity for cash to fund some of the inventory and assets, explaining that while the bank could assist in some areas, they would want to have personal guarantees.

Frank asked a number of questions regarding the funding, taxes, and guarantees.

The time passed quickly, and Brian got ready to leave first so the rest could talk among themselves.

As he reached for the door, Brian turned and said, "Keep me informed of your plans. Not just for your sake, but because I'm sitting on a new line of credit for Joe, and the bank can't do anything for him until all this is resolved."

"I don't understand," said Bob.

"Well, a line of credit is a risk to the bank. If you were all to leave, it would put Joe in a higher risk position. That has to be considered." Brian smiled, looked at the three, opened the door, and left.

The men nodded and spent a few more minutes talking about a few of the issues they had learned, and then Frank and Bob left together.

Brian's parting comment had caught Leigh a little off guard, so when he got a chance to leave the office midmorning, he called Brian and asked, "What did you meant about 'sitting on Joe's line of credit'?"

"I shouldn't have said anything," Brian responded. "But Joe applied for a loan a couple of weeks ago, and I'm still sitting on the application until this matter gets resolved. I could not expose the bank if you all quit. On the other hand, if you were to start another business right away and Joe couldn't get funding, that might be to your advantage." Brian knew he was saying more than he should, but the thought of being involved in another company to compete with Joe still excited him.

"Look, this whole thing is making me very uncomfortable. We all like Joe and don't want to see him get hurt. This all started over Betty and, well, I don't know, but it just doesn't seem right."

"I know what you mean, but this is not personal; it is just business. I can't be your partner and loan you money from my bank or I would. I think you guys are sitting on a golden opportunity here. If you need a silent partner, I think I could help you work something out."

"I think we are moving too quickly," Leigh suggested. "Let's see where this is all going first."

"I'm not trying to push you; you each have to do what is best for you," Brian answered and then added in his most concerned voice, "But if they let you all go, you should have a backup plan, and I could be a great deal of help, if you know what I mean."

"Yeah, I think I do. Give me a week and I will call you, okay?"

Brian agreed, and they said their good-byes. Leigh went to the coffee shop convincing himself that he was doing so to look for clients, but something was really bothering him.

THE CHAMELEON AT WORK ||||

Even after all these years Joe was amazed at how quickly Betty could get things moving if she set her mind to it. Over the next few days she talked to the Chameleon a number of times and made the arrangements.

She ensured that Joe had each manager agree to attend the Thursday night, Friday, and Saturday sessions and stay at the resort. She offered to pay them overtime for doing so or give them extra time off in lieu of the payment.

Leigh agreed instantly, opting for the extra time off. Bob agreed but took the extra pay. Frank was the most difficult to get to agree. He told Joe that he couldn't see what difference the sessions would make; he thought it would be uncomfortable and a waste of time and money.

Joe and Frank met in Joe's truck at one of the work sites. It was intentional. Joe wanted to see each of the men away from the office and didn't want to drag them into a coffee shop again. He thought that in the comfort of his truck the discussions would be quick and private. Frank, as always, wanted more detail than the other two. Joe explained the overview of the meeting and how everyone would go on line for twenty minutes in the days prior to the meeting to generate behavioural profiles for the sessions.

"I am not sure I want everyone seeing this test expose what it thinks might be a weakness," Frank said.

"That's not how it way it was explained to me. I was told that there isn't a right or wrong, good or bad, weak or strong profile. Each person brings something of value to the party, and each style has its challenges," Joe outlined.

"I think we all know that everyone has value," Frank replied and looked at Joe, who nodded silently in agreement. He did not respond so that Frank would feel compelled to continue.

"I mean, we know that Betty brings value to the company—that is not the problem." Frank paused before continuing. He wanted to choose his words carefully. After all, she was still the boss's wife.

"Joe, it is her meddling in the other departments and her constant questioning of what we do that has brought this to a head."

"Frank, I don't know if this will work or not but we, including Betty, are prepared to invest time and money to try."

It was Frank's turn to watch but not say anything, so Joe continued. "Betty still wants to be closely involved in the company, and I need her. But I can't afford to lose you guys either. Frank, I am in a tough spot, and all I am asking is that you come and see if there is any way we can work this out before any of us do something we later regret." Joe looked down, realizing he was becoming a little emotional; he did not want it to show.

"Joe, I owe you. You have been very good to me and given me breaks, so I will do it for you. I just don't think it will make any difference in the end." Frank put his hand on the door handle and looked over at Joe.

"That's all I want. Just come and see what this is all about. Then we can each decide where we go."

Frank nodded and opened the door. "I will be there Thursday evening."

Joe dropped into each office over the next couple of days and, with each manager, set up schedules with their next-in-command to manage Friday's workload so no one in the meeting would be disturbed.

A few days before their Chameleon Communicator workshop, the consultant had a phone meeting with Joe and Betty together and then separately to review what they felt the challenges were and how they could be resolved.

She also e-mailed them a worksheet on the real cost of conflict and asked them to fill it out. Then, together, they assessed the value and what were the different areas of concern.

The Chameleon also contacted each of the managers and asked them a number of questions about their department and asked if they could prepare a five-minute talk about it for the first evening.

Finally, she followed up by explaining the instruments that she would be using and asked each of the participants to complete a twenty-minute online survey.

Thursday evening, they all met in a small meeting room at the resort for a very informal get-together.

There was a great deal of tension in the air. Since the ultimatum, Betty and the managers had been avoiding each other except when absolutely necessary. Betty and Joe did not react as the managers gave their reports based on the questions they had been asked in regards to where they thought the company stood, where it was going, and what they could be doing better.

As each speaker finished, the Chameleon made comments, asked for clarification, and interjected a little humour into the process.

After all the managers finished their presentations, she asked Joe and then Betty to speak on how and why they started the company, some of their biggest challenges, and their best rewards.

By the time Joe spoke, the tension in the room had relaxed.

Finally, Betty spoke. Rather than just repeat what Joe had said, she shared some of the concerns and real fears she had in the beginning. She told the management team about how she felt when the one customer went broke and couldn't pay them, causing them to almost go bankrupt as well. She explained how that motivated her to keep on top of the receivables and not let anyone put them in that position again.

She shared how proud she was of Joe's building such a successful business and how committed he was to the quality of work and to the employees. She sounded a little awkward as she acknowledged the importance of the people in the room, but everyone could feel her sincerity.

The room remained completely quiet as she finished her talk, and the Chameleon broke the tension by summing up the talks and laying out the agenda for the morning. She then suggested that they relax and think about what they may have learned during this evening and they would all meet fresh in the morning.

The group went their separate ways in thoughtful silence … how had they worked for Joe and Betty for so many years and known so little about what it had been like for them to start out and go through difficult times? It certainly shed a different light on some of Betty's behaviours.

Friday morning began with the Chameleon Communicator explaining in detail the uniqueness of each person, each style. She explained how when we get an appreciation for differences in others, we can get along better. Finally, she explained how we could modify our own style, if only for a short period of time, to communicate more effectively with others.

She explained the system of colours:

- The Red spectrum measuring how people deal with problems and challenges
- The Yellow spectrum showing how each of us tries to influence others to our point of view
- The Green spectrum measuring how we respond to the pace of the environment and deal with conflict
- The Blue spectrum determining how individuals respond to rules and procedures set by others.

The introduction took about an hour, with the Chameleon telling a number of funny stories and examples around how the actions of the different behavioural styles play out in real-life examples. By the first break, the management team from Joe's Plumbing was chatting and laughing about some of what they had already heard. They were starting to recognize the styles of family and friends, and it was especially interesting when they thought about their spouses.

After the break, the Chameleon handed out the individual reports and explained how the first few pages give a general overview, in plain English, of how each participant reacts to the four areas of behaviour. Each participant read these two pages and then was asked to read a line they felt best summarized who they are.

The men looked at each other, but only Leigh waved his hand and said with a grin, "Mine says I am outgoing and like people. That detail really sounds like me, and I don't know how it could have come up with some of the statements based only on those few questions."

Betty looked up and said, "Mine says I am competitive, like to take charge, and speak my mind. That doesn't tell us anything new. I could have told you that without hiring a consultant."

The men looked at each other. Leigh rolled his eyes while Bob and Frank had to look down to keep from laughing.

The Chameleon then asked Frank to read a line, which he did, agreeing that it was accurate.

By the time they had gone around the table again, the group was loosened up. They continued to laugh at some of the content of their individual reports. They were all amazed at how different the reports were and yet how accurately they described each manager.

The next section outlined the value each person brought to the organization. The facilitator asked each to read the top three descriptors on the page.

Betty went first this time. "Mine says I am a bottom-line organizer, forward looking, and challenge oriented."

Leigh began reading his descriptors. "Mine says that I bring optimism and enthusiasm, practise creative problem solving, motivate others toward their goals, am a team player who negotiates conflicts ..." He would have continued down the full length of the page had Frank not cut him off.

"She said read three, not all of them."

"I know," said Leigh. "I just thought mine were so interesting that everyone would want to hear them."

The Chameleon laughed and asked Frank what his report said.

"Mine says I maintain high standards, I am conscientious and steady, and I am the anchor of reality."

"Bob?" the Chameleon prompted.

"I am a dependable team player," Bob said. "I work for a leader and a cause, and I am service oriented."

"That's similar to me," Joe said. "Mine says I am patient and empathetic, a logical step-wise thinker, and service oriented."

"Okay," the Chameleon said, "I want you to look at the dark side for a moment. Turn to the page that says 'Tendency Under Stress' and read what yours says. Bob?"

"It says I may appear 'non-demonstrative, unconcerned, and hesitant,'" Bob responded.

"Joe?"

"Mine is similar again with 'possessive, detached, and stubborn,'" said Joe.

"Mine says I can be seen as 'pessimistic, picky and overly critical.' I don't think that's right. I am just careful," Frank read.

"Wait a minute," Leigh jumped in. "When we went for lunch yesterday, who made us all change tables?"

"Well, I did, but the sun was shining on that table, and I thought it was too bright," Frank replied.

"And who sent their steak back to the kitchen?"

"It was undercooked. You can get sick eating meat that is too raw." Frank sounded defensive.

"And who disputed the bill?" Leigh was now obviously having fun at Frank's expense.

"I don't care if it was only off by twenty cents; it was wrong. People have to know when they do something wrong. It was as much for her benefit as ours. That is why I pointed it out." Frank continued to defend himself.

"So you don't think you are too picky then?" Leigh chuckled.

"I just have high standards and I like things to be done right. Doesn't everyone agree?" Frank could tell by the smiles as he looked around the table that they didn't. "You mean you guys think I am too fussy?"

"*Yes!*" came the voices in unison.

"Okay, Leigh." The facilitator brought them back on task. "What does your report say about your tendency under stress?"

"It says I can be seen as 'self-promoting, overly optimistic, and glib,'" Leigh said with a grin. "I can see how some people could come to that conclusion, except for the glib part. I just have a lot of valuable information to contribute, and I don't mind sharing."

The four now turned and looked at Betty, who was already reading several pages ahead of the group. She looked up and flipped back to the page they were on. "It says I can appear 'demanding, aggressive, and egotistical,'" she said and then added, "I don't like to be, but someone has to take charge here, and we have all the money invested, so I don't mind speaking out.

"Which brings me to the next section, called 'Possible Limitations.' My report says I 'overuse my position, lack tact and diplomacy, and take on too much, too soon, and too fast.'" She looked around the room, guessing what they were all thinking.

"I take exception to those statements, because we all know that Joe likes everyone and doesn't like to take charge, so someone has to. I don't lack tact and diplomacy. I just don't like to waste time and would sooner just get to the point." Betty sat back.

"Joe, what does your limitations page say?" the Chameleon asked.

"It says I 'yield to avoid controversy and I dislike change and dealing with diverse situations.' Which is why we are here, I suppose. I don't like conflict and wish everyone could just learn to be patient and get along."

"Ditto," said Bob.

"My report says I am inattentive to details, I can be unrealistic in appraising people, I trust indiscriminately, and I am a situational listener," Leigh said as a puzzled look crossed his face.

"And what part of 'list three things' did you not understand?" Frank said, only half joking.

"I thought that was only for the first list," Leigh said and then added, tongue in cheek, "I wasn't really listening." Everyone laughed.

"My report says I 'get bogged down in details, I am overly intense for the situation, and I appear somewhat aloof and cool,'" Frank said, reading closely. "Doesn't someone have to be concerned about the details?" He looked at the Chameleon.

"Concerned, yes, but there comes a time when you have to quit analysing and make a decision." Betty let her inside voice escape.

"You really are cool and aloof sometimes. Do you really think that way all the time?" Leigh asked. "I thought it was something I said or did."

"No. It bugs me when you come in all happy and excited and wanting to chat it up when there is work to do. I have a lot of responsibility in making sure my estimates are right, and it seems you don't take my work that seriously sometimes."

"Are you kidding? Selling your projects is so easy because your proposals and estimates are so exact and complete. Sometimes I just think you are too serious, and I try to lighten you up a little."

"And you still have to learn to make quicker decisions," Betty added.

"What is the consequence of Frank making a mistake?" the facilitator asked.

"You mean besides losing money?" Joe quipped.

"Yes, is there anything else?"

"Well, some of our work is around high-pressure vessels, and a mistake could cause something to blow up," Joe added.

"So, Betty," the facilitator said, turning to address her, "your profile is a lot like mine. I wouldn't have the patience to do estimates and check the detail of what is needed. If it were up to me, I'd make an educated guess and wing it."

"That is probably what I would do too," Betty said and then surprised everyone with a chuckle.

"Is that what you would like Frank to do?" The Chameleon was focused solely on Betty.

Betty grew serious again. "No, I don't suppose it is. It's just some of these things seem to take a long time."

"Betty, it sounds like the company would be at huge risk," the Chameleon continued, "if they had you or me try to do Frank's job. You need someone with his profile to take care of the details." She looked around the room for consensus, and everyone was nodding in agreement.

"It sounds like Frank is perfect for the job he does."

"I know I couldn't do it," Leigh said.

"In fact, it seems to me that most of you profiled very well for the job functions you have to perform," the facilitator continued. "I would be willing to bet that although some of you think Leigh is not serious enough during the day, he is out promoting the company and making sales calls in the evening when the rest of you are at home."

"So you agree with Leigh when he says that playing golf is in his job description?" Bob said with a smile.

"It could be if he meets potential customers. That is what this program is all about today. We are going to go through these reports in detail so you can better understand yourselves as well as each other. No one woke up this morning and said, 'How can I go about destroying everyone else's day?'

"We just have to better understand how we each think and work and what value it offers the team. Does that make sense?"

Everyone nodded.

"Good. Now let's break for lunch. It is going to be catered, so we can eat then go for a walk and meet back here at one when we will learn more and have some fun."

As the doors opened, the resort staff began pushing in carts with small sandwiches and beverages. Bob asked if they could keep talking about it through lunch.

"I am finding this really interesting," he said enthusiastically.

The Chameleon asked how the others felt, and when they all said they would like to just grab a few triangular sandwiches and continue, she agreed.

They were soon back at the profiles working their way through the 'Dos and Don'ts of Communication' for the various styles. There were quick glances and smiles shot around the room.

Joe noticed that even Frank seemed to be enjoying the session and that Betty was feverishly taking notes.

As they came to the first full-colour graph showing how each person was rated in all four dimensions, the Chameleon had to insist that they take a ten-minute break and all go for a walk outside to refresh their minds.

As they left the room, she noticed Bob and Leigh talking and laughing together. Betty and Joe wandered out slowly, and she could hear them talking about what they had learned.

Frank stayed in the room for some time and then asked the Chameleon Communicator if he could ask her a few questions about the reports.

"You can, but it must be while we are taking a walk around the grounds. Is that okay?"

Frank agreed, and they too left the room and were soon enjoying the afternoon sun as they strolled along the path down toward the lakeshore.

"I just love this location," the Chameleon said, looking around. "You are lucky to live near here."

"We are," Frank replied. Then he turned to the Chameleon and said, "I am finding this session interesting and fun but ..." He hesitated for just a split second, but it was enough for the Chameleon to jump in and finish the sentence.

"But what validation studies do we have?"

Frank stopped short, looked at her, and said, "Yeah. How did you know what I was going to say?"

"The reason I don't give you the reports ahead of time is so we can all explore them together. I find that more effective. However, I do review them all before I come here, and this is what I know about you."

She quickly reviewed his core colours. "As you now know, the Blue being your highest," she said, "means that you like to follow the rules, you worry about making mistakes, and you study the detail."

They discussed the reports in more detail, and she explained again that these reports were about behaviour and how they measure *how* we do things, not *why*. She explained that she had other reports that identified motivators and values or the *why* people do things.

"Will we be doing the motivator reports as well?" Frank asked.

"Normally I would, but this was set up too quickly, and we do not have time. Hopefully it is something we will do later.

"Combining the two reports tells us more about who we are. For example, from talking to Joe and discussing those first questions with you, I suspect you have a high theoretical score, meaning you have a thirst for knowledge."

"Well, I do love to learn. Seems like I am always reading or taking extra courses on something," Frank responded.

"Knowing that, I knew you would want to know more about this program and your high Blue style would want the detail. So I figured that you would want proof of what I am telling you. Is that right?" She smiled at him.

"Wow. That about sums it up. If Joe and Betty ask me about the motivator course, you will have my vote." Frank laughed and was impressed, but he still wasn't convinced that this would solve the problem at hand.

For the balance of the day, the entire management team reviewed where everyone was in the four dimensions of behaviour. They compared their similarities and differences in how they solved problems—the high Reds going right to the heart of the problem and dealing with it directly to the low Reds avoiding dealing with the problem. They compared how some people convince others by virtue of their enthusiastic nature (high Yellow) and how some people convince based on logic (low Yellow). They noticed how the high Greens like to start something and finish it before moving on and the low Greens are the consummate jugglers. The high Blues like to know what the rules are and expect everyone, including themselves, to follow the rules; the low Blues think the rules are for others to follow.

Then the Chameleon placed on a large circular graph on a flip chart stand.

"This shows how the reports measures 384 different combinations and then create this graph that reveals each person's unique style and compares them to the rest of the team."

She explained in more detail the independent validity studies that rated the accuracy of the results while Frank jotted down a number of notes.

She then repeated what Joe had grown used to hearing: "There is no right or wrong, good or bad style—each person offers something different to the organization, and a strong organization should have a variety of styles. You can see from this chart that this organization is well balanced with the five of you all spread around the wheel."

"What questions might you have at this point?"

Frank had a couple of minor questions regarding the graphs, and Leigh said that he was really enjoying the day. There were no other questions, so the Chameleon looked at her watch. "It's 4:30, and we are right on schedule. I would like us to stop for today. I believe that Joe and Betty have arranged for us all to have dinner at 5:30 in the main restaurant."

The three managers headed to their rooms to freshen up. Joe and Betty stayed behind to debrief with the Chameleon.

Saturday morning they started the day with a great breakfast on the patio. Joe looked around, expecting to see the old man, whom he had not seen or talked to for several days. At the end of their last meeting, he had told Joe that he had to go away for a few days but expected to return soon.

Joe noticed that the group was laughing at some of the quirks each style had when dealing with the others. He had not heard them laugh together in some time, and it made him smile and even relax a little. As Frank was quizzing the waiter on the menu, he heard Leigh say, "Why don't you turn down the Blue and just order the special?" Joe realized they were using some of the neutral Language of Colour and understood what the old man had said about them learning to communicate without words loaded with emotional attachments.

Later, while Betty was monopolizing the conversation and talking over the others, Bob, who usually observed quietly, said, "Perhaps you should turn the Red down a little." She turned to him and then laughed, as they all understood the message. Betty, Joe realized, did not feel insulted or threatened. This was worth every penny.

After breakfast, they gathered back in the room to start the second day by reviewing how each person fit onto the wheel and why together they formed such a well-balanced team. They talked about how they were stronger than a less-diverse group and what each person could do to communicate more effectively with the other members.

The Chameleon explained the difference between behaviour and motivators as she had done briefly with Frank and said that was something she hoped they could visit at a later time.

At the end of the day, the facilitator went around the table and asked each participant to explain in their own words what they found most valuable and how they intended to use that information back in the workplace. The laughter they had shared over the past couple of days made it obvious to all of them how much they had actually enjoyed each other's company.

After the program finished, both Joe and Betty approached the Chameleon Communicator and offered their heartfelt thanks.

"I have a feeling that things will work better now, but there is still a lot of work to do if we want to build on today's success," Joe said.

"Now that I understand their styles, I will try to move a little slower and turn the Red down a little when I am dealing with them," Betty added.

"And I think they will be a little more aggressive and open when communicating with you," the facilitator replied, "now that they understand it is your style and there is no need to take things so personally.

"I have promised to work with the managers individually and with some of the employees they have challenges with over the next month. I think we should get together and plan other strategies so it all ties together."

Betty agreed.

Monday began with a renewed energy, but by noon Joe had a new problem on his hands.

DISSECTING THE CHAMELEON

Tuesday morning Joe met with the old man out on the deck, and after a quick exchange of greetings, the old man asked, "Well, how did it go?"

"For the most part, the retreat went well. Betty, Frank, and Bob have found some common ground and, more important, a common language that they can use to communicate. They agreed to expand the training to the rest of the employees and to be less critical about each other.

"I think they now see the strengths each brings to the job. It will take some ongoing coaching, but I think it is going to work. But you won't guess what happened at the office yesterday when we got back."

"Leigh quit?" the old man said.

"Now, how did you know that?"

"Just a guess. I felt he was in the wrong job from some of the comments made earlier. Often people recognize that at a retreat and decide to make a change."

"That is the part I don't understand. He did fairly well. But why were his sales not higher? He was a core Yellow—an outgoing, friendly, talkative, and convincing person. It is going to be hard to find another person like that. Our other salespeople have some Yellow, but I think their core colours are Green, and if you can believe it, I think one is Blue.

"I don't know how we could have made that mistake. I now know that successful salespeople should be high Yellow—a good talker with enough Red to make them aggressive and competitive." Joe sat back and looked at the old man for some reinforcement.

"Wrong. A good salesperson should be a good listener and problem solver. They should be able to ask good questions. A good talker will often buy the product back before the client has time to buy it in the first place," he said with a smile.

"So knowing a person's colour doesn't help with identifying how successful they will be in sales?" Joe questioned.

"Knowing the behavioural style of a person will tell you how they behave, how they will sell. That is good information for hiring a salesperson, but more important in measuring sales success is to know *why* they behave as they do. You might say this is a measurement of their motivation."

"The Chameleon said she wanted to talk to us about that later. What exactly do you mean?"

"Take Leigh, for example. I think with his behavioural style and his skills in asking good questions he will do well in sales, but not for your product." The old man stroked his beard.

"Now for sure I don't understand. Leigh knew our products; he was well liked, good with the clients, and seemed to know everyone in town. I thought he would make a lot of money. Why was he not more productive?"

"From what you told me about Leigh, my guess is he's motivated by social or aesthetic causes. Does he have another job to go to?"

"Yes. He has been offered a position as a fund-raiser for the local art gallery. What are you thinking?"

"The behavioural profiles you did will tell you a lot about how your salespeople will sell. I would bet the fellow you said was Blue does well with contractors. He probably knows all the specs and technical information and does very thorough presentations."

"He sells fireplaces or heating systems based on their efficiency and plumbing jobs based on the low cost of ongoing maintenance using the fixtures we're providing or some other mathematical value," Joe said, thinking out loud.

"This salesperson probably has a strong businesslike relationship with his clients," said the old man. "The Green salesperson probably sells better to end users and makes presentations based on the higher comfort your heating designs provide or the low hassle of your plumbing designs.

"The Green salesperson probably does a lot of repeat business and services the heck out of the repeat clients. Does that sound a little like them?"

"As a matter of fact, you got it. So if any style can sell, how do you know who would be successful?"

"The profiles you did measured the *how*. To find the *why* or the motivation a salesperson has, you need to measure their values."

Joe responded quickly. "Betty and the Chameleon talked about doing a values program next, but I thought it was about sales and having high moral values, which we insist on."

The old man nodded sagely and continued. "I understand what you are saying, but that is not what she meant by values. Psychologists agree that there are six key values or motivators, as they are also called. Like the four core behaviour styles, the higher we score on each of the values, the more that value motivates us."

"I am not sure what you mean," Joe said.

"Briefly, the Chameleon will introduce you to the six values, which are Theoretical, Utilitarian, Aesthetic, Social, Individualistic, and Traditional. She uses a questionnaire similar to the one you did for the behavioural profiles, only it measures the *why* of a person's life—what propels them into action." The old man waited for Joe's response.

Joe thought for a moment, writing in his notebook, and asked, "What are those values again?" The old man repeated them slower as Joe wrote. When he was done he clicked his pen off and said, "So is this similar to the behaviour profile in that there is not one style but an infinite combination of all six?"

"Exactly, and by looking at the three values that are furthest from the national means, you can more accurately predict what will motivate that individual and propel them into action." The old man smiled.

"Just how is it you know so much about all this?" Joe asked.

"I have been through these courses a number of times at work and find them very interesting," the old guy responded.

"You know, all this time I assumed you are retired and never asked you what it is you do or did." Joe was feeling a little embarrassed as they had now had many conversations, but they were always about Joe and his problems.

He was beginning to realize how little he really knew about this mysterious old man.

The old man just smiled. "I work for a bank," he said, adding, "the same bank you use here in town. But I work at the head office."

"What is it you do there?" Joe sat up, trying to remember if he had said anything too embarrassing about the bank.

"Oh, I am just a problem-solver." The old man said.

"Maybe you can look into my problem and find out why I still don't have word on my loan." Joe laughed as though he was being funny, yet the comment carried a seed of seriousness with it.

"Sorry, but unless you have borrowed millions and can't pay it back, I wouldn't get a look at your file. I trust you do pay your loans back." Now it was the old man's turn to let out a small laugh.

"Anyway," Joe said, "getting back to this values thing. If I had a tool to tell me what motivates a person or why they do things …" He paused as he collected his thought before continuing, "and if I understood their behavioural or communication style, I could really control my employees."

"This isn't about control," the old man responded. "But if you understood that much about your employees or clients, how would be advantageous to your business?"

"If I understood what motivates people as well as how they will do it and how they will communicate with others …" Joe paused, grasping the implications, the excitement shining in his eyes, "it would eliminate many of the challenges I have as a leader."

"You are beginning to understand." The old man smiled.

"So tell me about these six key values and what they mean," Joe prompted, intrigued with the prospect of new insight.

"The facilitator will take a full day to explain and review the values with you and your people, but I will give you a brief overview.

"Participants who score high on the Theoretical chart have a deep interest in learning. They tend to read a lot and will be more motivated by the opportunity to learn than by other values such as money."

"I thought everyone was motivated by money." Joe said.

"If one of your employees is high Theoretical, a new learning opportunity is a reward. If an employee is low Theoretical and you 'reward' them with a course, they wonder what you think is wrong with them."

The old man looked at Joe for agreement before continuing, but Joe replied sceptically, "I find that hard to believe. It seems to me that everyone is motivated by money."

"That is one of the assumptions many businesspeople make, because successful businesspeople tend to score high on the Utilitarian scale. This scale is a measurement of the desire for a return on their time, their money, and their resources. Validation studies have demonstrated that commissioned salespeople will have Utilitarian as one of their top three values, and it is something that, as an employer, you should be looking for when hiring a salesperson.

"The problem is that we tend to think that everyone is like us. We think if money motivates us, then money should motivate everyone. The truth is that the world is full of examples of people motivated to do jobs for reasons other than money."

"I have never heard this before," Joe said.

"For example," the old man continued, "I know of one young woman who gave up a good corporate position to accept a similar position for less money at a university because she was high Theoretical. She was motivated to accept the new position because of opportunities she felt it offered in learning benefits. To her, that was more important than the money."

"Okay," Joe said slowly, dragging it out. "I can see that. I have a friend who could be making a lot more money but instead has worked for a nonprofit for years. I could never understand why." Joe shook his head, still not quite getting why someone would choose to work for less money.

"He is probably a high Social person," the old man said. "Social issues or causes motivate these people more than money, and thankfully, we have them."

Joe nodded his head in agreement and said, "I can see how that would not be a quality for successful salesperson."

"Not necessarily." The old man grinned. "Think of a situation where success in sales was good for a social cause."

"Selling Greenpeace memberships." It was Joe's turn to grin.

"Exactly!" The old man laughed. "A salesperson who cares about raising funds to further a social cause can still sell; they just won't be doing it for their own financial rewards. Understand?"

"I get it but, what about the other values?" Joe said, looking down at the notes he had scribbled on the wrinkled page in his pocket notebook.

"People who score high on the Individualistic scale like opportunities to be a leader. They work well on their own, and this too can be a good trait for people in sales. Especially if they have to work on their own outside the office." The old man hesitated for a moment and then continued.

"People with a high Aesthetic score are motivated by beauty and harmony. If that is coupled with a high Utilitarian score, then you have a salesperson who might be great at selling fashion items, artwork, music, or any product that has or enhances beauty. Does that make sense?"

It was as though a light went on in Joe's head. "It does. That's Leigh. He was always going to concerts and art shows. I think I'm seeing the relationship between values and behaviour and how they complement each other," Joe said. "Tell me what the last value, Traditional, is all about."

"Traditional people are folks who may resist change. They like making decisions based on a defined view of life. They tend to belong to organizations that have hierarchy, like religious organizations, the military, police or fireman, and other traditional institutions."

"Wow." Joe half breathed the words as he thought. "This is even more interesting than the behaviour workshop."

"It can be," the old man continued. "Like the behaviour profiles, we each score somewhere on a spectrum for each of these values, and it is the combination of all the values that gives different motivation to each of us. We tend to find it easy to talk with people who share our values. That is why many of your friends may be other business owners."

"Well, we do have the most in common to talk about. A lot of people just don't understand the problems with business—they think it always easy and profitable," Joe said.

"But think about why you are all in business. What values do you share?" They continued the discussion of another half hour, and every time the old man answered a question, it seemed as though it brought two more to Joe's mind. It was as though he couldn't get enough, like a new door was opened and he saw the opportunities that this would give him in hiring and managing his people.

"I think I understand, and before I hire a new sales manager, I will profile the candidates for both behaviour and values and then decide which person is the best to hire," Joe said.

"Partially correct, but for the profiles to have any value, you should benchmark the job first so you know what to measure them against."

The old man went on to explain how the benchmarking process was done and how the behavioural and motivator profiles should only make up about one-third of the hiring decision. He explained to Joe how one-third should be on the interview process and references and one-third on their training and experience. They continued to discuss how a conscientious manager might use tools for those areas as well.

"I am just a plumber trying to make a living, and suddenly this seems all so complex. How do I acquire the skills to do all this?"

"Joe, I believe I told you before: you are no longer a plumber; you are a businessman, and the more you know about these ideas, the more successful you will become.

"Those who plan and profile their people profit." The old man went on to explain how it begins with a benchmark, the standard against which something can be measured or assessed, and how many companies hire for a position thinking. "If we could just have someone like Sue or Andy or Joshua, they would be perfect for the position!" The old man said, then went on to say that they compare people to people. He explained that to remove the bias of thinking about people for the job they had to begin thinking about the job itself.

"The question we should ask is 'If the job could talk, what would it say?' What kind of authority and responsibility does the role have? What kind of decision making is most effective in this role? What performance objectives will success in this role be measured by? This helps us to define the key accountabilities for the job itself, not the person."

"I can see how having a system all worked out would sure help. Often I get into an interview and I don't even know what to ask. We end up talking about the local hockey team, and if I get a good feeling, I hire the person," Joe observed.

"Trust me; you are not alone. Most people, even the most successful businesspeople, do the same thing. That is why I suggested that you get someone like the Chameleon on your side. Compared to the cost of hiring the wrong person, a good consultant is cheap."

"There are more things to think about than this, but again, this is something the Chameleon can help you with. Clearly defining the job to begin with will help avoid 'the romance of hiring.'"

"Romance?" Joe looked at the old man with a smile.

"There is a tendency to get carried away by personality, other relationships, and whatever else causes us to hire people that don't fit.

"You would not install a furnace or a hot water tank that did not meet the client's specifications, so why do we hire without even knowing the specs of a job?"

"I have found this process most fascinating," Joe said. "There is almost too much to remember."

Again, the old man continued telling Joe to get help preparing a clear definition of what the role is responsible for and how it will be measured. Then, as qualified candidates are interviewed, they are asked to complete surveys that assess them in the key accountabilities for the role. He explained how the Chameleon prepares a report that compares the job to the people and told Joe that he would find it hugely interesting because he could see at a glance who can naturally do the tasks and the motivators required for successful completion of the job. He explained how everyone involved in the hiring process has to do thorough interviews and reference checks and develop a total talent management process.

"If, for example, you had done this for Leigh's role, I think you would have determined that the job of sales manager called for someone who was motivated by both money and leadership opportunities. You would have found out early on that Leigh's passion was in the arts, not in plumbing contracts. That is just one example; it is far more complex than that, but that gives you an idea."

"So we should benchmark all jobs in the company?"

"You can. You would want to benchmark key roles like service manager, controller, and so on, and you could benchmark to define the key accountabilities for service technicians and work toward hiring to that standard." The old man looked at his watch. He caught the waiter's eye and asked him to bill his room. Joe protested, but the old man said it was his turn to treat and would hear nothing of it.

As the two men waited for the waiter to return, they looked around the complex, and once again the old man told Joe how fortunate he was to live in such a great location.

Joe agreed but was only half listening. His head was feeling as if it would explode with all the new information, but he was eager to keep learning. *If I could just get a better handle on our people*, he thought, *then most of my challenges would be gone.*

Joe grew quiet as he looked over some of his notes and then said, "This all sounds complex and expensive."

"Actually, once you have set up a system for hiring, you will find it makes the job easier, and compared to the expense of hiring the wrong person, it's cheap." The old man slowly got up from his chair, and Joe knew that signalled the end of their meeting. The younger man rose and escorted the elder to the front door.

The old man smiled. "I have to leave again for a few days. Can we get together next Monday?"

"I'll be here," Joe said, thinking, *Why does he ask me? I am the one getting the benefit of all this wisdom for free. This old fellow seems to really know his stuff.*

Watching the old man disappear through the door, Joe wondered why he had never before encountered the vital information he was learning. He wondered how the old man knew so much about it. *I must remember to find out more about him on our next visit,* he thought.

THE BANKER'S VISIT ‖‖‖‖‖‖

Three days later as Joe came into the office, he heard Betty call out to him.

"Joe, I got a strange call this morning while you were out," Betty said. "A man named Will Buterman called and said he was with the bank and made an appointment to visit us this afternoon."

"Is he coming with Brian? Maybe they finally approved that operating line we've been waiting for."

"No, that's the funny part. He asked me not to mention it to anyone, especially Brian, right now. He is doing some sort of customer service audit and just wants to ask us a few questions."

"You're right. That does seem strange."

It was precisely 2:30 when Will Buterman arrived for his appointment.

"Show him in," Joe told the receptionist. "And tell Betty that he is here, would you?" Joe closed a file and quickly straightened his desk.

Will was a short man but seemed big in presence as he entered the room. He shook Joe's hand vigorously as Betty walked in and introduced herself, and then the three of them sat down.

"I will get right to the point," Will said. "I understand that you recently asked for an increase in your line of credit."

"Yes, and we are anxious to get it as we have a plan to expand the retail sales," Betty said.

"I had a quick look around your store on the way in. It looks good," Will said.

"It does," Betty agreed. "Joe is great at making the place look good, but you were looking at most of the inventory since we carry little backup. That means that every time we sell a fancy tub, we have to either order one in for the customer or else take apart the display. We have room for more inventory at the back and would like to be able to offer quicker service to our customers."

"That makes sense. How long ago did you apply?" the banker asked.

"For the loan? It must be close to six weeks now, but you must have record of that," Joe said, nodding toward the file Will was holding.

"I am not in the loan department. I am just doing a customer survey with some of our long-term business clients and your name was drawn, but I don't have your loan details. Did Brian tell you that he is waiting for additional information from you, or is there something that you are aware of that could be preventing approval of the loan?"

"Nothing," said Betty. "I gave him everything he asked for with the application. Our past few years have been good, and our debt-to-equity ratio is low."

"May I be frank and be assured that this conversation will not leave this room?"

"By all means," Joe said. He was alarmed now and leaned forward as if others could hear through the walls.

"The bank got a disturbing call from someone who suggested that we question you and Brian. The caller said that Brian offered to be a partner with someone if they became your competitor. He also said that Brian was sitting on your loan application knowing that without the loan, a new company would be more competitive."

"I can't believe that. Brian has been our account manager for years, and I think he takes good care of us." Joe looked at Betty, who for once had nothing to say.

The banker continued. "We take an accusation like this very seriously, but before we do anything, we like to talk to the people involved to see if there are any grounds to the claim. We can find no evidence and do not want to have someone slandered, and that is why this must be very confidential."

"We certainly understand that," Betty said. "Can you tell us who made the call or how would he would know what is going on?"

"I can't tell you who called, but he was in a position to know something, although he is no longer in that position. He may be just trying to cause trouble. We have reviewed all our files and can't see anything suggesting that Brian has done anything wrong, but we have to look into it, and as the accusations involve your business, we thought we should ask you about it as well," Will explained.

"We understand, but this is all new to us," Joe muttered, barely able to get the words out.

"I am sure it will probably turn out to be an oversight on someone's part, but we feel it is important to check these things out," Will said in a more reassuring tone. "I will be meeting with Brian in the morning, and although I can't guarantee you we will issue the loan, I can guarantee that we will review it and get back to you this week."

The man rose, shook both Betty's and Joe's hands again, and left without further discussion.

"Wow! What was that all about? I wonder what Brian's up to. I hope he didn't do anything wrong."

"Joe, you're so naïve. Just because you like someone doesn't mean he likes you. Haven't you noticed how jealous he's been of you the past few years?"

"Jealous? There have been many days when I wished I had his job. Who do you think called the bank about all this?" Joe asked.

"Maybe it was Leigh. They did golf a lot, and he may have gotten some inside info."

"I can see that," Joe said. "Leigh has a high set of moral standards, and he knows a lot of what is going on. If he thought it was wrong, he'd turn Brian in."

"Well, at least we will have this matter dealt with one way or another. I understand that Leigh will be raising money for the art gallery. Maybe we should make it one of the charities we support." Betty looked at Joe.

"I take it you don't mind that we spent a lot of money training Leigh for someone else?" Joe asked her.

"I always knew this wasn't a right fit for him," Betty answered. "I'm sure this will work out well for him and us both. Besides, there's no reason not to have him still singing our praises to everyone he meets on this new job."

ALL IS QUIET ||||||||||||||||

In the office, there seemed to be more harmony and a new respect between Betty, Bob, and Frank. The odd tense moment still surfaced, but when it did, they took a minute to address it. Betty was much more patient and empathetic, while Bob spoke up more often at the weekly meetings, just as the Chameleon had suggested.

Frank, who had been the most vocal in calling for the removal of Betty, was working toward having more empathy, and the two remaining salespeople had picked up the slack left by Leigh's departure.

Betty had been spending time one-on-one with the Chameleon, so she understood the motivators and how to use them and the associated tools for all their hiring procedures. Now she was talking about developing complete strategies and succession plans as well. Joe wasn't sure about all the time this was taking, but he knew that the receivables were now at thirty days instead of forty-five. A few other small changes had been made, and overall, they seemed to be making more money with a lot less hassle.

As promised, Will Buterman had called from the bank's head office within a week to say that the loan delay had been a misunderstanding at head office and the line of credit had been approved.

He also said that the calls about Brian were malicious and had no merit and in fact he was being promoted to head office as well.

A new account manager was being transferred in, and Brian would bring him around for an introduction.

A much more relaxed Joe continued to spend the occasional morning at the resort with the old man, who introduced him to the new resort manager. They began talking about buying the Mastermind program from Max-U and forming a group. Joe also asked about renting a meeting room for possibly running the programs "Selling with Style for Nonsalespeople" and "The Art of Listening for Better Results," which the Chameleon and Betty were discussing.

The new manager told Joe that he was aware of the programs and would be interested in possibly sharing the programs with Joe's company if he wanted. The old man assured them both that that would be a good idea and a great investment.

When Joe arrived at the resort one morning, the old man was not there. While it was unusual for Joe to arrive first, he thought little of it and opened the morning paper.

A few minutes later a waiter came out, set a book and a glass of water on the table, and said, "I'm sorry, sir, but your friend has been called away suddenly. He said to give you this book and tell you he would be back in the fall and would like to discuss it with you then."

"That's it? That's all he said?" Joe felt empty. He looked forward to their morning talks, and although they had spent so much time together over the past weeks, he realized that there was still so much he didn't know about the old fellow.

Joe asked if the new manager was in his office but was told that he was out of town as well. Joe ordered his usual toast and coffee and then picked up the book and looked at the cover. It read *Get Out of Your Way: How to Use Self-Hypnosis to Remove Your Limiting Beliefs*.

The old man had talked about this book and promised to give him a copy. As Joe thumbed through the pages, an envelope fell out. He picked it up, opened it, and read the few lines that were handwritten inside.

I am sorry I had to leave so suddenly, but some unfinished business came up and I have to deal with it. I will explain when I return. In the meantime, enjoy the book, and we will talk about it when I get back. Thanks for your assistance in helping me make some tough decisions of my own.

Joe finished his breakfast and paid the bill, but he still felt a little empty as he headed back to the shop.

For the next few days, he arrived early at work and buried himself in things he had been putting off for some time. He still missed his trips to the resort and having breakfast in the early morning sun, so one morning he walked into Betty's office and said, "Grab your jacket. I have something I want to show you."

"What is it?" Betty looked up but made no effort to move.

"I'm not going to tell you. I said I have something to show you. Now grab your jacket and come on."

Betty wondered what was going on. *This action seems a little "Red" for Joe,* she thought. As they made their way along the winding road by the lake, she realized that it had been quite some time since she had just sat in the passenger's seat and looked out the car window.

Joe escorted her to the deck of the resort and pulled out a chair for her, saying, "Please be seated. Your waiter will be with you promptly."

Betty laughed as they both sat down and said, "What are you up to?"

"Nothing." Joe grinned. "I just think it's time we begin to enjoy the treasures we have, and I can't think of anything better than spending a couple of mornings a week having breakfast with you, here in my favourite spot."

Betty smiled as she picked up the menu and decided she would have a fruit dish. They spent almost two hours talking about the family, the business, and future plans, something they hadn't discussed in some time.

Two or three mornings a week they did the same thing, enjoying their breakfast and making new plans. They discussed the new direction they wanted to take and evaluated what to do with the profits that seemed to be increasing monthly. They talked about how much easier it was to run the company. They decided so much of it seemed to be falling into place in line with the complete strategy they now had in place.

As the weeks slipped by, both seemed more relaxed and laughed often. Joe began taking Betty by the hand after breakfast and walking her down to the edge of the lake, where they just gazed out at the beauty of the scenery.

One morning as they stood on the shore, Betty turned to Joe and said, "I don't know what has changed, but I feel closer to you now than I have since we were young."

Joe laughed and told her she was still young and then added, "I don't know what is different either, but we do seem to talk more and at a deeper yet more relaxed level." He smiled and added, "Does that make sense or sound a little esoteric?"

"Esoteric? What kind of language is that for a plumber?" Betty looked at him and laughed.

Joe loved the way her eyes lit up when she laughed. He had really meant the comment about her still being young. *Technically we could be considered middle-aged,* he thought, *but she looks as beautiful as the day I first met her."*

"Sewage-lagoon isn't the only big word I know." He smiled down at her. "I read the other day that if you add a word a day you can improve your vocabulary considerably within a year. I thought I'd try, just for fun."

"I love you, Joe. I love the old fun-loving you who seems to be back." She squeezed his hand and looked at him with her eyes smiling. He felt warm inside and knew what she meant by her comment of feeling closer.

"Somehow I just feel more relaxed," he said and turned to head back up the hill, Betty still in tow.

The regular breakfast meetings seemed to be half planning sessions for the business and half dates where they just took time for each other. Both soon looked forward to the next meeting and in no time had a regular schedule of going to the resort every Monday, Wednesday, and Friday, and they never missed, as nothing was more important in their minds.

One morning, as Joe was saying his greetings to the resort manager, Betty picked up the morning paper, sat down with her back to the warm stucco, and began to read the business section. When Joe returned, she folded the paper and slid it across the table.

"Look at this article. It says that our old bank manager, Brian, has resigned from the bank. Strange that he would accept a transfer and then quit so quickly, don't you think?"

Joe picked up the paper, and the photo seemed to jump off the page. He stared at it for a long moment and then in disbelief read:

The president of the bank, Jim Johnston, returned from a three-month hiatus from an undisclosed location where it had been rumoured that he was recuperating from personal health issues.

"The old man I had breakfast with is Mr. Johnston, the bank president," Joe half mumbled, still staring at the photo. Betty, deep in thought, did not seem to hear him, and Joe began to read out loud as he still stood beside the table.

Mr. Johnston said his absence had given him time to reflect on the future direction of the bank. He said that he had several meetings with "a brilliant young businessman," whose name he would not disclose, who had inspired him to propose some changes to bank policies. The bank will be offering more programs to small businesses.

"Joe," Betty interrupted, "don't you think it's funny that Brian would take the transfer and then quit?" Pausing briefly, she added, "Do you think there is more to the story?"

Joe nodded, only half listening as he read the last line from his old friend.

In our desire for rapid growth, we had forgotten the small business partners who originally built this bank. We had forgotten some of the human side that small business has to deal with. We forgot that you can't fire your friends, partners, or wife. We forgot the old adage that you should "dance with the gal who brung ya." We forgot about the small businesses that brought this bank to where it is today. They are the gal who brung us and, thanks to my new friend, we are going to start dancing with them again."

Joe put the paper down. "Did you see that? A bright young businessman?"

"What?" Betty was still thinking about Brian. "I'm sorry. I was just wondering why Brian quit, and I didn't hear you."

"The old man that I met mornings, the one that gave me the idea of the Chameleon and so much other advice—he is the bank president."

Joe sat down still in disbelief as he slid the paper back across the table and pointed to the bearded man in the photo.

"No way!" Betty said. "That was the guy you were meeting with all those mornings?"

"He called me bright!" Joe said in disbelief.

"You are bright, Joe." Betty's tone changed to the softer voice she mostly kept reserved for him and the girls, and she continued, "And the only one who doesn't see it is you."

Betty looked at the article again. "Joe, he credits you with changing his thinking just the way you credit him with changing yours. It just proves that it doesn't matter who you are or what your position—everyone has challenges."

She took Joe's hand in hers. "That is why I love you."

Joe smiled. "I just don't believe it."

"You don't believe I love you?" Betty sat up smiling as she mocked his last comment.

"No. I just never suspected that the old man was anything but a friendly old man. He is responsible for building a large international bank, and he is crediting me with helping him."

"I guess that is what the Chameleon meant when she said, 'It doesn't matter what colour your behavioural style is, what motivates you, who you are, or where you come from. We all have something to learn and teach others. And most important of all, each of us can achieve what we believe is possible.'"

EPILOGUE

Joe and Betty did continue to be successful in both the business and life. The division managers continued to learn and grow with the business, and over the next few years, they expanded it into more branches in neighbouring towns.

As the company grew and became more profitable, so did the managers' salaries and bonuses. Leigh did an outstanding job as a fund-raiser and was truly enjoying life in the arts community he so loved.

Brian invested the small settlement offered him in a restaurant, but it failed in year three and he had to take a job as a mortgage broker.

As promised, the old man returned on a regular basis, and he and Joe had many more interesting breakfasts on the deck.

We would like to end the book with "and everyone lived happily ever after," but this would then be a fairy tale rather than an example of life.

In the next book, Joe and Betty face new challenges, as Joe is involved in a near-death accident and realizes that he has to make a clear succession plan.

JUST THE FACTS, MA'AM

"The facts, ma'am; just the facts."
—Famous quote by Detective Joe Friday

The story of Joe was of course just that, a story. Any similarity to real people or events is purely coincidental, except of course for a few friends who make guest appearances, and you know who you are.

The tools used in the book are based on behavioural psychology. They are real and provided to industry and commerce by TTI (Target Training International Ltd.) and used by the real Chameleon Communicator™, Myrna Park. Myrna uses these tools in a number of ways, including those very similar to how the Chameleon and the old man used them in this story.

By using a story format, we hope that we have been able to present this material in a way that has made it fun to learn. In future stories, we will also be showing how the Chameleon Communicator, Max-U Inc., Myrna, and Layton use these and other tools to effectively assist clients in dealing with people problems, succession planning, improving leadership skills, and making businesses run more efficiently and profitably.

If your organization needs a "round-up from the ground-up," call Max-U for more information on how to improve the performance and attitude of the people in your business, 1-877-312-MAX-U (6298) or talk to the person who gave you this book.

Recognizing DISC

DISC is the universal language of observable human behaviour. Scientific research has proven that people, in terms of "how they act," universally have similar characteristics that can be grouped together into four quadrants, or styles. The DISC model analyzes behavioural style; that is, a person's manner of doing things.

DISC behavioural psychology was developed based on the work of Dr. William Moulton Marston (1893–1947), author and co-author of five books, including *Emotions of Normal People* (1928). DISC is popular in business today and is used to understand how we function in the four areas of normal human behaviour.

Defining DISC allows us to "compartmentalize" the four distinct behavioural styles. As we gain understanding of the styles, we begin to see others differently and appreciate the differences. When we learn to adapt our behaviour to each of the styles ("be a chameleon"), the effectiveness of our communication increases, allowing for greater understanding and appreciation of our similarities and differences.

The colours used in the story are the colours of the charts and graphs used by TTI and make remembering the styles as described by the Chameleon in the story easier to remember.

These four behavioural styles are:

D – Dominance (RED): how you handle problems and challenges
HIGH RED—Tendency to be very active and aggressive in gaining results. Will go directly at the problem with little or no fear.
LOW RED—Tendency to go at the problem with calculated, organized, well thought-out approach to gaining results.

I – Influence (YELLOW): how you interact with other people
HIGH YELLOW—Tendency to have high contact ability, social, outgoing, and very verbally persuasive.
LOW YELLOW—Tendency to be more sincere, reserved. Enters situations and relationships with more of a cautious approach. Fact and information oriented.

S – Steadiness (GREEN): how you handle a steady pace and work environment
HIGH GREEN—Tendency to prefer a more structured, predictable environment, having boundaries of the "pond" clearly defined. Prefers a secure situation.
LOW GREEN—Tendency to prefer an unstructured, undefined environment with a great deal of freedom to operate.

C – Compliance (BLUE): how you respond to rules and procedures set by others
HIGH BLUE—Tendency to follow rules set by others and is very aware of the effects of not complying with rules and procedures.
LOW BLUE—Tendency to do it "my way," establishing their own rules.

The four dimensions are often shown in a grid with the "D" (Red) and "I" (Yellow) sharing the right side and representing extroverted and optimistic aspects of behaviour and the "C" (Green) and "S" (Blue) on the left side, representing introverted and pessimistic aspects of behaviour.

"D" (Red) and "C" (Blue) then share the top half of the grid and represent task-focused aspects of behaviour and "I" (Yellow) and "S" (Blue) share the bottom half, representing the people-focused aspects of behaviour.

 Recognizing DISC Styles

C COMPLIANCE

The "C" is looking for: Information

Emotion: Fear

Quick Observations: Introverted, task-oriented

Communication: Direct

Overextension: Critical

Body Language:
Stance - Arms folded, one hand on chin
Walks - Straight line
Gestures - Very reserved, few or no gestures

Communication Clue: Asks detailed questions

D DOMINANCE

The "D" is looking for: Results

Emotion: Anger

Quick Observations: Extroverted, task-oriented

Communication: Direct

Overextension: Impatient

Body Language:
Stance - Forward leaning, hand in pocket
Walks - Fast, always going somewhere
Gestures - Hand movements while talking, big gestures

Communication Clue: Doesn't want others' opinions, only facts

S STEADINESS

The "S" is looking for: Security

Emotion: Non-emotional

Quick Observations: Introverted, people-oriented

Communication: Indirect

Overextension: Positiveness

Body Language:
Stance - Leaning back, hand in pocket
Walks - Steady, easy pace
Gestures - Will gesture with hands

Communication Clue: Has a "poker" face

I INFLUENCE

The "I" is looking for: The "Experience"

Emotion: Trust/Optimism

Quick Observations: Extroverted, people-oriented

Communication: Indirect

Overextension: Disorganized

Body Language:
Stance - Feet spread, two hands in pockets
Walks - Weaves, people focused, may run into things
Gestures - Big gestures and facial expressions while talking

Communication Clue: Talks with hands

061209

How to Recognize the Styles

	(D) RED	(I) YELLOW	(S) GREEN	(C) BLUE
Nature Symbol	Fire	Sunshine	Forest	Water
Emotion	Anger	Optimism	Stoic	Fear
Pace	Fast/Clipped	Fast/Energetic	Slow/Easy	Slow/Measured
Priority	The Results	Interaction	Relationships	The Process
Orientation	Tasks	People	Family/Group	Work
Need to	Control	Verbalize	Accommodate	Follow Policies
Irritated by	Inefficiency Indecision	Boredom Routine	Insensitivity Impatience	Surprises Unpredictability
Eye Contact	Intense	Scattered	Empathetic	Reflective
Posture	Forward	Animated	Relaxed	Restrained
Voice Speed	Fast/Clipped	Fast/Energetic	Slow/Easy	Slow/Measured
Appearance	Businesslike	Fashionable	Casual	Formal
Work Space	Formal	Cluttered	Personal	Structured
Under Stress	Dictate/Assert	Sarcastic	Submit	Withdraw/Avoid
Seeks	Productivity	Recognition	Attention	Accuracy
Gains Security by	Control	Flexibility	Relationships	Preparation
Wants to Maintain	Success	Status	Relationships	Credibility
Support	Goals	Ideas	Feelings	Thoughts
Change	Likes It	Indifferent	Time To Adjust	Concerned
Likes You to Be	To the Point	Stimulating	Pleasant	Precise
Wants to Be	In Charge	Admired	Liked	Correct
Measures Personal Worth by	Results Track Record	Recognition, Compliments	Depth of Relationships	Precision, Accuracy
Decisions Are	Decisive	Spontaneous	Considered	Deliberate

To really engage and be able to absorb this material quickly and easily, it would be helpful if readers used a highlighter or crayon to colour the different columns in the respective colours.

While there are numerous companies who offer DISC assessment tools, TTI is one of the world leaders in online assessments (www.ttiassessments. com). As consultants, one of the benefits we have seen from the TTI assessments is the use of positive terminology. Although the assessments acknowledge "the dark side" that accompanies each style, TTI assessments are true to the foundational belief that "all styles have value."

TTI invests significantly on research (a reflection of a High Theoretical Value as an organization). The independent validation studies of these tools have proven that the accuracy of these instruments is extremely high.

The research shows how we are not made up of one style as often described in quick tests that claim someone is a driver (D) or a communicator (I), amiable (S) or analytical (high C) but rather a combination of all styles as they relate to each area being measured. In this way, rather than dividing the population into four groups or sixteen as some instruments do, the TTI instrument has almost four hundred different combinations. These can then be plotted on a graphic wheel. This allows us to get a visual representation of the different behavioural styles of group members. This shows group tendencies (the behaviour of the team) and helps to explain why some group members may have good relationships with each other and why they may be in conflict with others.

Both authors, Layton and Myrna Park, are experts in DISC analysis, and their business involves helping leaders and managers use these tools to understand themselves and their employees and why they behave as they do. It is also helpful in predicting how employees will respond to different scenarios in the future.

The program "Selling with Style" shows salespeople how to use this DISC information to see clients' styles and understand how they should communicate or present to them most effectively and close the sale. High Reds (D), for example, will only want the executive briefing: "Just give me the big picture and show me the bottom line" is often their preference. The High Yellows (I) will want to know what great new relationships and how much fun will come out of this sale. The High Green (S) will resist change and do their best to avoid any conflict that could arise from the sales process. The High Blue (C) wants to see all the detail, the specifications, and what the back-up studies show and will run through all the scenarios before making a decision.

DISC has also been used to establish safety programs in the workplace. DISC assessments have been used for pre-employment screening to predict which individuals would have an increased likelihood of experiencing on-the-job injuries. When the use of these assessments is combined with education and a structure that enhances the transmission of safety-related information and reinforces safety through a reward system, organizations achieve a higher level of safety performance.

This is, of course, a very brief overview, but can you begin to see the benefits of understanding the people we work with and sell to?

So, if you are

- **High Red:** Take it from me that you will love the results to the bottom line.

- **High Yellow:** Trust me—you will love this and find it a lot of fun.

- **High Green:** We can send samples so you can see the benefits clearly.

- **High Blue:** We can send you more detail and copies of validation studies.

Author Biographies

Layton Park, 1949–

Layton graduated with a diploma in architecture in 1970 and began a design/build company in the spring of 1975. By 1986 he had over eighty employees and several subcontractors working for him.

A lifelong student of psychology, he has studied with many of today's leading teachers of mind and mental toughness and founded the Canadian Hypnosis Institute.

Layton became a business analyst and, along with Myrna, has focused primarily on consulting to businesses for the past fifteen years.

Layton has written four other books and writes much of the material they both use. This is the first joint effort by Layton and Myrna, and they plan to follow up with at least two more adventures of Joe and Betty dealing with business.

Myrna Park, 1958–

Myrna graduated from the University of Alberta with honours and then founded a real estate company at age twenty-six. She quickly built it to a major competitor in her market as well as becoming a lead instructor for the provincial licensing courses.

After joining Brian Tracy International as an associate in 1999, she switched her focus to working with businesses to improve their people and their communication. She believes that "to build strong organizations, you must first develop strong people." Myrna is a skilled facilitator for many of the leading programs on the market. She is known throughout Canada and the United States as the "Chameleon Communicator ™".

Most recently, Layton and Myrna finished a series of workbooks for facilitators and participants for change, leadership, conflict, and performance management.

Max-U.com

In the past five years we have expanded our companies and continue to focus on our business clients in order to determine exactly where they are, where they want to be, and the best way to get there.

We would like to thank you for reading the story of Joe and remind you that leading any organization requires constant growth. We hope this has given you some insight into the types of tools and training available and that you will follow Joe and Betty in the success of their business.

Layton and Myrna Park
1 877 312-MAXU (6298)
www.chameleoncommunicator.com

Business References for Myrna:

MYRNA PARK ON STAGE IN LOS ANGELES WITH THE AUTHOR
OF *CHICKEN SOUP FOR THE SOUL*, MARK VICTOR HANSEN

Myrna has guided us through this strategic planning process for several years now, and I am always impressed by the professional way she goes about getting our group to focus on what is the task at hand.

She can take a planning situation that starts out with very complex problems with divergent interests and create a process and guide the group to simple and often creative results.

The important part is the results, because at the end of the day you need to have a plan going forward, and she gets that.

—James A. Paterson, Partner
Pushor Mitchell LLP
Lawyers

Myrna brings a wealth of experience and understanding to our strategic planning process. Strategic planning has been described as "herding cats," and she masters this process beautifully.

With her understanding of the governance nature of organizations, she keeps the group on track, focusing on the strategic activities of the board and not bogged down in discussions about day-to-day operations.

—Weldon LeBlanc
Chief Executive Officer
Kelowna Chamber of Commerce

I thought the training was amazing. First, Myrna is amazing. She is easy to talk to and understand and has many great ideas. I think it is very valuable to my current role in regard to dealing with people, customers, and staff. It is also very beneficial to my personal life. I think the topics are relevant everywhere.

I've always thought of myself of being positive, but the course brought a new perspective to it. I now try to turn things around when something doesn't go quite the way I thought it would. I don't only do that for myself; I do that for the staff or at home for my family

I do want to thank you and Capri for sending me to this course. I think it has made and will continue to make a huge impact in my life.

—Tracy Hackl
Capri Insurance Services Ltd.
Commercial Vehicle Department

I enjoyed the class and found the information quite useful. I would definitely recommend this course to other team leaders and young rising stars in the company.

—Denise A. Dendy
Team Leader
Capri Insurance

Business References for Layton:

Layton Park is one of the most dynamic individuals I know. I value the experience and knowledge Layton has to offer me in life and in business. I am grateful for is his guidance in some of my most important business decisions.

Layton's quick wit and sense of humor always puts me at ease and enables me to view things from a different perspective.

—Karna Germsheid
Owner, BAM Media Inc.

Layton is such a wonderful and fascinating man. He has helped me with my business (and life) more than words can even say. He is very knowledgeable and personable with high integrity, and I would recommend his services to anyone looking to improve their professional or personal life.

—Troy Mitchell
Troy Mitchell Enterprises
Speaker/Trainer

I met Layton at an event in Las Vegas a few years ago and found him to be very professional. Layton has an incredibly unique ability to phrase everything in a very straightforward manner, and he can add humor to it so not only is it knowledgeable to read but enjoyable as well. He is intelligent, efficient, professional and witty, which makes him an incredible joy to work with and a great positive person to be around.

—Audrey Nesbitt
National Marketing Coordinator,
Online Marketing Director at Brown, Koro & Romag, LLP
Los Angeles, California

Layton is a multi-skilled professional, which allows leadership and feedback to be gained from both book and experience. His lightheartedness and humor make working with him truly enjoyable.

—Desmond Regier
Owner of Trade Exchange Canada

I'm not a fan of the "see you at the top, you can do anything, go get 'em" approach to life and work. Layton embodies that energy and resourcefulness but without all the rhetoric and empty cheerleading. His energy and quick mind are infectious.
—Layne Longfellow
Owner, Lecture Theatre, Inc.
Prescott, Arizona

I have known Layton for many years. Our first connection was during a college instructor development training program, and later I co-facilitated a personal development workshop with him. Layton is the real thing. He is a "what you see is what you get" kind of person. He is caring, warm, competent, and genuine and takes a keen interest in the well-being of his clients. I am pleased we have remained friends for all these years and would highly recommend him as a consultant and or coach.

—Michael Douglas
Instructor, Okanagan College

Layton is a fabulous author, and I am happy to endorse his books and programs focused on the power of our minds. If you are looking to remove or change your limiting mental roadblocks and make improvements personally or in business, I recommend you book an appointment with Layton.
—Melonie Dodaro
President and CEO, MindBody FX
Weight Management Company Inc.

I wish to express you the gratitude for your book You the Success Generator. *It has strongly helped me with my life. I became more liberated and became more self-assured, overcoming the complexes. I began to look more positively at life in general and all that waits for me in the future. I have already presented your book to several friends in hopes that they too will turn out as I have.*
—Michael Komarov
Russia

You made an unbelievable impact on the volunteer trainees! There were several comments after regarding your way of speaking, which brought an incredible peace to several of the trainees and me.

You are an absolute delight! A few suggested that your presentation should be oh-so-much longer than it was. We cannot possibly thank you enough for the impact you make just by being you!

Thank you! Thank you! Thank you!

—Shirley Buchanan
Palliative Volunteer Services
Central Okanagan Hospice Association

I have known and done business with Layton for over thirty years. We have faced good and bad economic times together, which has given me a great perspective on how Layton carries on business under various conditions.

I admire his ability to maintain his sense of humor and positive outlook as well as his constant search for new courses, methods, or way to succeed during these times.

Layton is very creative and has a mountain of business experience to call on, making him valuable as a consultant or business coach. If you need a fresh perspective on your business or marketplace, add Layton to your team.

—Kevin Dale, Partner
Wayne Building Products
Edmonton

**Contact Max-U.com for additional references or
booking information for either Layton or Myrna
1 877 312-MAXU (6298)
www.chameleoncommunicator.com**

Books by Layton Park

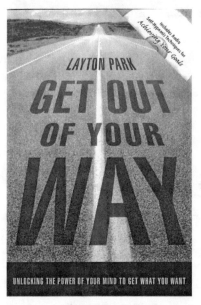

Get Out of Your Way
Unlocking the Power of Your Mind
to Get What You Want
Or, How to Remove Limiting Beliefs
Through the Power of Self-Hypnosis
Discover what beliefs or fears are
holding you back and how you can
change them and succeed in your goals.
Trade Paperback 9780738710525
6 x 9; 216 pages; Published March
2007 by **Llewellyn**—New Worlds of
Body, Mind & Spirit

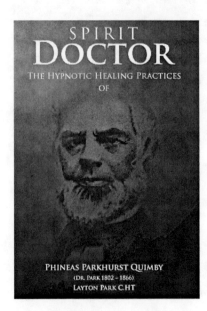

Spirit Doctor
The Hypnotic Healing Practice of Phineas
Parkhurst Quimby
(Dr. Park 1802–1866)
This is the story of America's most
influential hypnotist, spiritual mind,
and father of new thought.
A man responsible for numerous
healings using practices and methods
scientifically explained by Dr. Bruce
Lipton in his book, *The Biology of*
Belief.
Published by: iUniverse
ISBN 978-0-9732111-3-9
6 x 9; 109 pages; Published 2010

Books by Layton Park

If You Are Going To Lead ... Don't Spit!
This book is a collection of motorcycle stories from Layton's humour columns in the *Busted Knuckle Chronicles*. The lessons in leadership in each story remind us that leaders are everywhere and are instrumental in everything we do.

Published by iUniverse
ISBN 978-0-9732111-5-3
6 x 9; 81 pages; Published 2010

Communication Tools for Any Trade
Layton Park and Myrna Park
A Simple Blueprint For Getting Along At Work
This compelling business parable is about a tradesman who, together with his wife, builds a very successful business. That is until the day the three division managers tell him he has to make a choice between them and keeping his wife involved in the business.

Published by iUniverse
ISBN 978-1-4759673-4-0
6 x 9; 120 pages; Published 2010

Books by Layton Park

Chicken Coop ... for a Rubber Sole
This book is a collection of stories from Layton's columns in *North of Fifty*. These humorous stories are great short reads, ideal for airports or traveling where you may want to enjoy something light and fun. This book is an ideal inexpensive gift that can be easily re-gifted and enjoyed by people of all ages.

Published by iUniverse
ISBN 978-0-9732111-6-0

Don't Drink the Kool-Aid
How big business, government, and religion use hypnotic techniques to influence their followers.
This book, scheduled for release in Spring 2013, is a "must- read" for anyone wanting to position their organization in the minds of their customers and employees or wanting to understand how other big institutions are doing so to them.
Advance orders are available from the publisher in quantities of twenty for only $200 plus shipping.
Contact info@max

CPSIA information can be obtained at www.ICGtesting.com
Printed in the USA
LVOW130114260313

325948LV00001B/34/P